THE
ENGLISH LAKES

FRONTISPIECE. *The southern end of Lake Windermere, looking north*

The
ENGLISH
LAKES

By
Frank Singleton

Illustrated from
Colour Photographs by
WILFRED ELMS

London
B. T. BATSFORD LTD

To
SIR NORMAN BIRKETT
True Son and Lover of the Lake District

First published 1954

MADE AND PRINTED IN GREAT BRITAIN
PHOTOGRAVURE PLATES BY CLARKE AND SHERWELL LTD.,
KINGSTHORPE, NORTHAMPTON
TEXT PRINTED, AND BOUND BY JARROLD AND SONS LTD., NORWICH,
FOR THE PUBLISHERS B. T. BATSFORD LTD.,
4 FITZHARDINGE STREET, PORTMAN SQUARE, LONDON, W.1.

CONTENTS

ACKNOWLEDGMENT

I AM everywhere indebted. For more than thirty years I have been visiting the Lake District and am still but a tiro, a beginner, compared with many. Yet I could not resist the invitation to write this book and I am grateful, above everything, to the publishers for the freedom they have allowed me. I have tried to meet their requirement that the reader should be offered as informative a book as space allowed and they have in turn encouraged me to make it readable in my own way. Mr. Brian Batsford and Mr. Sam Carr have been consistently encouraging. I do not attempt a bibliography but in the introduction I have given details of the books that among many others have particularly helped me. From them I have quoted freely and for permission to do so am indebted to authors and publishers; the Rev. H. H. Symonds, Mr. Bruce Thompson, Miss Doreen Wallace, Mr. John Betjeman, Mr. Norman Nicholson, Mr. W. H. Auden, Mr. Cecil Day Lewis, the Rev. C. M. L. Bouch, Messrs. Sherratt and Hughes, Mr. Rupert Hart-Davis, Miss Margaret Lane, and others.

In the preparation of the manuscript I have been greatly helped by my colleague Mr. Frank Morris, and Mr. A. Hazelwood of the Bolton Museum Department who read it. Mr. F. J. Carruthers, editor of the *West Cumberland Times* gave me much expert information from his local knowledge, Mr. David Curnow has been continuously stimulating, particularly about Fletcher Christian, Mr. Stuart Hayes read the proofs and Mr. Victor Tonge compiled the index. I am endlessly indebted to my wife, in particular for her diaries of our journeyings.

The photographic illustrations are eloquent for themselves without words.

F. S.

LIST OF ILLUSTRATIONS

All the subjects were taken on Kodachrome 35 mm. film

9

Introduction

HOWEVER many books about the Lake District there were yesterday, this book is the latest today, November 11th, 1954. Of tomorrow I cannot speak. There is no last word on the subject. There is no best book. The material is constantly changing. Even such things as we thoughtlessly call permanent—the mountains and the lakes themselves—either change, it may be into mines or reservoirs, or our knowledge of their nature and origin changes. Writers, as persistently as painters and photographers, strive to record the scene and story as they seemed in their day. If the author is true to his own fresh vision and skilled enough to express it, he may feel, even among all the crowded shelves of second-hand books in Mr. Varty's shop in Ambleside, that his own book is unique. And F. H. Bradley has told us that every sunset, were it conscious, must think itself immortal, because it is unique. I have written my own book without I hope falling into the error of the hypothetical sunset.

It says as much as the allotted space would allow of what I wanted to say about the Lake District in the middle of the twentieth century. Over sixty years ago Baddeley, in the most authoritative of the guide books, commends the classic dignity and repose of Haweswater where the inn "The Dun Bull" has "lately been enlarged and now offers very fair accommodation". He strikes the contemporary note when he says of Thirlmere: "At the time of writing, the countryside about here is terribly disfigured by the progress of the Manchester Waterworks. The defacement arising from chimneys and spoil-heaps . . . and the smoke nuisance . . . would certainly not be excused in Manchester itself. We write of Thirlmere as it is in 1891." In our day we take

Thirlmere for granted but can tell the story of Haweswater.
To the great tradition of lake poets we can add Mr. Norman
Nicholson; to the other denizen writers many from Beatrix
Potter to Sir Hugh Walpole. A century ago Whitehaven
had already outlived the fame and prosperity which had
followed the inventions of the eighteenth-century engineers—
coal-mining beneath the sea, the steam-pump and steam-
engines, coal-gas, railways. On ground where Romans and
monks as well as British shepherds trod, the engineers
flourished and faded—for a time. Everything is for a time
and in our day we may turn a speculative eye on the architecture of the plutonium factory at Sellafield, and adjoining
it at Calder Hall, Britain's first atomic power station. Will
that scene a century hence have a period flavour? Will there
even be another century? Contemplating what used to be
accepted as the everlasting hills and the sea, we may, or
may not, like Mr. Cecil Day Lewis, find it "amusing to
think" that

> a piece of jelly which came from your maw
> some aeons ago, and contracted a soul,
> may atomize earth and himself and you—
> Yes, blow the whole bloody issue back into the blue.

In addition to material so new it would have startled our
forebears, there is, surprisingly, always something new about
what one might lightly assume to be done with. The closed
chapter must be opened, or a new one inserted, to tell the
story, for instance, of Mr. C. S. Wilkinson's fascinating
detective work in his book *The Wake of the Bounty*, in
reconstructing the history of Fletcher Christian. It leaves
one persuaded that Sir Herbert Read is probably right in
thinking that Wordsworth's story has even yet not been
fully told. There are still gaps in what we know about the
years in France. Wordsworth could be clam-like in secrecy
and managed even posthumously to impose reticence. After
all, more than six people knew about his association with
Annette Vallon, but it was over a hundred years before the
story "got out". There may still be more to come, as there
has been about his school-fellow who led the mutiny. There
is, too, the pleasure of being surprised by discoveries in what

one has assumed to be familiar territory. In addition to
their exploits in the air, men

> in bells of crystal, dive—
> Where winds and waters cease to strive—
> For no unholy visitings,
> Among the monsters of the Deep:
> And all the sad and precious things
> Which there in ghastly silence sleep.

That "sad" is exquisite. How many even among Words-
worthians would have guessed the author? "To Enterprise"
(of all subjects!) was late vintage, written when he was over
fifty.

But however much is new, the most and best are inevitably
old. It is deeply satisfying to come to this countryside "as
to a known place". It can never be so known that we cease,
in our brief day, to have eyes to wonder. Tongues to praise
are more tricky. After thirty years I still see the Lake
District as for the first time and I have tried to express that
vision as freshly as it is vouchsafed. Inevitably, in writing
of a district so steeped in literary associations, there are
innumerable echoes and overtones. I accept that. This book
is full of good things—by other people. Some have written
so well. It is the others who, if vigilance nods, will slur the
words and blur the vision. One has to read so many books
in which the relevant facts nestle under prose that is like
coloured cotton wool. They "hie on . . . where yon . . . if
aught . . ." Histing and harking they breathe on the clear
pane. On the first page I open, that great and good man
Canon Rawnsley, begins: "Yet listen I pray you for sad is
the tale of Lyulph's Tower . . ." The useful and ubiquitous
Arthur Mee can hypnotize one . . . "Dunderdale Blackey has
little but that little is much . . . a stone water-pump of which
legend has it that Queen Mab herself . . . but they are friendly
folk in Dunderdale Blackey." Yet are any of us the lords
and masters of our phrases all the time? One of the most
astringent writers I know, after describing Harrison Ainsworth
as a tripe-hound, concludes his chapter: "But you shall carry
the tang of witchcraft with you."

On the other hand, few districts of comparable size can

have inspired such good writing as the Lake District. Apart
from the poets, those who have written practical guides
seem to have flexed more than their muscles in grappling
with the subject. There is a sort of toughness about the
thought and language that can at times be formidable. I do
not attempt a bibliography, but among those who have long
been my companions, and to whom my debt is immeasurable,
a handful are outstanding. Wordsworth's *Guide to the Lakes*,
published originally in 1810 and last re-issued by Rupert
Hart-Davis, edited by W. M. Merchant in 1951, is a poet's
admirable prose, compact with thoughtful generalizations
and apt detail. How fortunate we are that in our day
another poet, Mr. Norman Nicholson, has written one of the
best of all regional books: *Cumberland and Westmorland*
(Hale, 1949). He is a man of the rocks, knowledgeable,
deeply responsive, realizing that all that constitutes scenery,
or the surface of the earth, has its explanation in the nature
of what lies beneath, and he tends to look there first for the
descriptive clue even when his subject is the poet Wordsworth ... born on limestone, reared on sandstone ... Skiddaw
slate analogous to the plain, bold verse of the experiments,
volcanic rock to the soaring poetry of Tintern Abbey and
then the Silurian characteristics of the long years of anti-
climax. It was the poet in Mr. Nicholson thought up that.
The Lake Counties written by W. G. Collingwood, illustrated
by A. Reginald Smith (Warne & Co.) first published in 1901,
re-published frequently, added to by friends, and corrected
at the publisher's invitation by members of the public, is a
classic, perhaps *the* classic, "a darlint book", and the despair
of successors. Here the note of authority, common to all I
am going to mention, is the quietest and perhaps the most
impressive. One feels proud to belong to The Cumberland
and Westmorland Antiquarian Society which under him,
and his famous son, R. G. Collingwood, and other eminent
figures like Chancellor Ferguson and Bishop Ware, Mr. and
Mrs. Hodgson (they deserve a chapter to themselves, the
names so crowd forward). Graham, McIntyre, Simpson,
Canon Wilson, and others achieved so much and made this
eighty-year-old local society famous across the seas. They
opened up the sources of local history and archaeology and

the note of almost unconscious authority in W. G. Collingwood, which I was really out to capture when led into this
digression, is noticeable in his reference to the fact that in
1889 this local society set out to explore what many could
not believe to be the ruins of a Roman fort. "So it was
determined by the local Antiquarian Society to explore. In
the north tower we found a gem-ring, spear-head, and key,
showing that the site was Roman and worth more attention,
and digging was carried on until 1894." The end result,
after many setbacks, was the excavation and re-creation,
still in progress, of Hardknott Castle, most inspiring of
Roman remains in the district.

Among all the writers, Baddeley is of course the oracle,
the Bible, the omniscient. Encyclopaedic, he is to most of
us authoritative to an unassailable degree. Whatever he
despises I would never dare to hanker after. He has only to
pronounce a peak inaccessible and I shall not attempt it.
Him I have honoured in his place, his last resting-place in
Windermere. One too like him, tameless, and swift and
proud, as one might perhaps reprehensibly put it, is H. H.
Symonds. *Walking in the Lake District* (publisher Alexander
Maclehose, London, now W. & R. Chambers, Edinburgh),
is the supreme book on that aspect of the subject. Not only
does it contain every conceivable piece of practical information but it enables the reader to share the free play of an
adult and educated mind on a great theme. I have hardly
ventured, in this book, into Symonds' territory, expecting
readers to find their own walks if the general characteristics
and other things are adequately indicated. Any kind of
what might be called expert walking should be done under
the guidance of Symonds. You may unexpectedly be
belaboured with a Greek quotation when negotiating a
difficult bit. You must comfort yourself with the thought
that this man can even stand up to Baddeley. On Esk
Hause, we read, cliffs, combes and ridges are all characters
of the great Apocalypse. "And there is bog . . . too, in these
high places (quite avoidable by knowledge) and mist on
some days, and a certain tracklessness, and the wildness
seems to have shocked the nerves, or wet the feet, of the
far-stepping Baddeley: for he is brief here, and apprehensive,

and inadequate." It is as if, suddenly, quietly, one tiger bared its teeth at another. It goes in one place a stage further. Symonds actually takes a nip. Or so those of us must feel who know that after generously acknowledging that Baddeley "could write and could walk . . ." Symonds adds, "Yet he kept to the end in some ways just a touch about him of Aunt Emma." Yet everywhere even the qualifications imply the essential achievement. After describing what it is like along the top of Crinkle Crags, for instance, "high places where you can hear the trumpet tones of the precipices and, at the same time, the quiet harmonies of a softer land at your feet," Symonds goes on: "Though along the mile-and-a-half of Crinkles you should not walk star-gazing, for it is a place all gnarled and gashed by old earth movements which split and ground the strata and gave cause, even to the lion-hearted Baddeley, to short-circuit some of the sixty-seven (is it?) separate tops of rock. . . ." And of the supreme Ennerdale walk, eastward from Crag Fell to Pillar Fell he writes with mounting enthusiasm: "You are going with a great panorama to delight you: you are high up: you walk to a climax, a fifth Act, and you are original, for you will beat Baddeley—a rare conquest: this walk missed him."

I have indicated the quality of my chief guides and companions. I tremble to think what any of them would make of my book. Still, I accept the insight of André Gide when he said: "What another would have done as well as you, do not do it. What another would have said as well as you, do not say it; written as well, do not write it. Be faithful to that which exists nowhere but in yourself—and thus make yourself indispensable." We are none of us that, as we know, but the way there is wisely recommended. But enough of method and manner. Let us get down to the facts; to rock bottom.

Wordsworth cared nothing for geology and when he felt that his *Guide to the Lakes* needed it he wisely asked Professor Sedgwick to contribute. Nobody cares more for it than Mr. Nicholson, the outstanding Lake District poet of our day, and though many guides are admirable, to nobody better can the reader turn for an intelligible, indeed absorbing,

Looking east-north-east from the ☞
summit of Orrest Head

account of the story of the rocks. From the facts about
them he distils poetry, even a certain mystique. Miss Doreen
Wallace gives perhaps the clearest elementary guide through
the unimaginable tracks of time. H. H. Symonds is more
extended and stimulating at the level of the Headmaster's
Sixth Form. Our more modest aim will be like that of great
Baddeley himself to point out those differences of formation
which have a visible effect upon the scenery.

The most difficult concept for the amateur in geology to
grasp is that of time. It all happened so long ago. How long
ago? The expositors vie with each other in simple images
to help us. "Longer ago than . . . oh longer ago than that . . .
well longer ago than . . ." and I shall fall back on the phrase
with which as children we used to cap such contests and
shout victoriously: "Longer ago than you can say or think!"

Well, that long ago, there was laid down in fiftieth parts
of an inch, over many millions of years, the deposits of
sediment that under pressure became rock. Eventually we
shall know this rock as Skiddaw slate. Skiddaw and Saddleback are typical of the mountains made of it—rounded, big-
shouldered. Whilst this so-called slate still lay beneath the
waters, there came up from the molten interior of the earth
volcanoes, no doubt up into the air, but in any case throwing
up molten stuff which fell back on to the submerged Skiddaw
slate to a depth of ten to twenty thousand feet, gradually
filling up the shallow sea bottom which then sank and was
filled up again. Falcon Crag near Keswick is everybody's
favourite bit of volcanic rock, perhaps the very plug from a
volcano's throat. But the grandest scenery, the most rugged
and varied of the district, is volcanic. To it belong not only
the giants of the central massif but the great and lesser fells
in an oblong, thirty miles by eighteen, lying lengthways
from slightly south of west to north of east, clearing the
southern end of Derwentwater and the northern end of
Windermere. Practise your eye on the outlines of the
Helvellyn range, the Langdales, Glaramara, Scafell and
Great Gable and you will learn to recognize the nubbly,
craggy, humpy volcanic rock scenery not only of Bow Fell
but of the last little fling of that giant of the centre at the
sea-end of the diminishing range that forms the eastern side

of the Duddon valley in Bank End near Broughton, where volcanic rock joins all the others that go to make up the sands of the shore.

During the period of the eruptions one main point may have been in Borrowdale, for nearby, direct flows of lava are recognizable. So the name is used for all volcanic rock in the district.

In the course of our narrative we are still under the sea and still sinking and rising till the sea is shallow and contains corals and shell-fish whose remains begin to drop and mingle with ashes from the volcanoes, and you may still trace their fossilized remains in what is called Coniston limestone. Then in another deepening of the sea the increased pressure on a new deposit of mud made the Silurian Rock—the third of the main divisions of Early Rocks: (1) Skiddaw slates, (2) Borrowdale Volcanic (here Coniston limestone intervened), (3) Silurian.

The typical Silurian landscape is the wooded countryside of Windermere and Coniston. We have the key to the scenery as we know it, though all is over-simplified, all is still under the sea, and all is going to take longer than you can say or think to emerge.

Whilst our instructors are struggling to help us with images of layers of black and grey and blue cloth, or apples baking and furrowing like landscape, or sheets of paper crumpled into a ball, I fall back on what still remains, in many ways, the only adequate account. "And God said . . . let the dry land appear: and it was so. And God called the dry land Earth; and the gathering together of the waters called He Seas." And if His ways seem inscrutable now, how much more so must they have seemed then because, according to the scientists, having risen, it all sank again, and rose and sank again and for the third time rose. And perhaps it was the third time the author of Genesis (who like all writers on this subject was limited for space and knowledge) was referring to; for after unimaginable inter-action of sea and storm and sky it was earth: not yet our earth, for there was so much still to come before we came, granite and coal, and the ice age. Wonderfully the geologists manage the story, and having read them I fall back on another recollected childhood jingle. What, in effect, seems to have been the course of events was:

> First it rained and then it blew,
> then it frizzed and then it snew
> then it rained and blew again
> then it frizzed and snew again.

I don't see how we are going to emerge from these happenings except as children or molecules. Anyhow it was none of our doing.

How gratifying, when one shows the moving film to the family in the darkened drawing-room, the way one can whizz through what got in between and come to the interesting bit. So must we if we are to cover the ground, so let us whizz on and suddenly, there on the screen, is Scafell Pike.

What are the facts? For now it becomes our responsibility to marshal them. Scafell Pike is the highest point in England. It rises to a height of 3,210 feet. It is composed of volcanic rock, is frequently capped with snow, commands an extensive view of surrounding mountains. Those are unassailable facts. Thus for centuries Scafell Pike looked out alone. Then primitive man must have come—whizz the film on a bit— Stone Age, Bronze Age, Iron Age . . . suddenly our era . . . slowly, please, century after century, count in hundreds, sixteen, seventeen, count in tens. The years have twelve months now. Find October, find the seventh day, stop! There is Scafell Pike and we can add a new fact. There is Wordsworth on top of it. The story of Scafell Pike would be absurdly incomplete if it omitted that. And what Wordsworth made of it and what we make of him are also part of the story. Nor will it end there. In no time compared with what the mountains took to make they seem to be peopled. There across the gap is Carlyle on Great Gable, trying to capture the view in a thunderous phrase or two for *Sartor Resartus* which will then rumble off all the more effectively perhaps to do a great deal of harm in European politics. There is Mrs. Edgworth on Skiddaw, and Keats and Southey. And here approaching is Dr. Arnold with young Matthew. There is no end to it. The Lake District, as they say, has many literary associations.

E.L.—2

Many books have been written on this aspect alone. Mr. G. S. Sandilands compiled a substantial and fascinating anthology of passages in prose and poetry about Lakeland life and landscape (Muller). Canon Rawnsley filled two fat volumes with literary associations and stopped sixty years ago. Merely to glance through his chapter-headings is to see more names than even the syllabus of the English Tripos could expect one to know—Coleridge, Wordsworth, Lamb, Southey, Shelley, Gray, Ruskin, Rogers, Turner, Keats, Carlyle, Tennyson, Charlotte Brontë, Mrs. Hemans, Miss Martineau, the Arnolds, Emerson, de Quincey, Scott, Rossetti, Mrs. Gaskell and many others. It would be easier to list the absentees. Where is Oscar Wilde, where is Queen Victoria? The figures in the landscape are like one of those pages crowded with vignettes of all the characters in one of the novels of Dickens. (Where, by the way, is he?) Clearly we can give no complete account. Nor will we let the distinguished throng oppress us. After all, this is our day. Yet I am constantly refreshed by some of the unexpected glimpses—Harriet Martineau nipping out before dawn, a swift thirty or forty steps in the nude, to that cold slate bath, the first in the district; Tennyson, resting on his oars on Windermere, gazing into the unruffled water whilst he quoted his own lines from "Morte d'Arthur". "Not bad, Fitz . . . is it?" The tiny figure, not more than five feet high, in a black silk gown, thin, with brown hair, expressive eyes, big mouth, bulging forehead, sweet voice, Charlotte Brontë advancing across the drawing-room at Brierley Close to shake hands with Mrs. Gaskell; the mail coach that in 1840, as a newspaper reported, travelling at a rattling pace hit a gig with great violence at Ruffa Bridge and knocked it into the adjoining field along with the horse, part of the wall, and the two Mr. Wordsworths—"the venerable and highly esteemed bard and his worthy son". The only damage was that the v. & h.e.b's finger was scratched. Such glimpses present themselves with a sudden vivid authenticity as when in boyhood I first watched in a Windermere hotel one animated little old lady entertaining two others. I was told she was Lady de Freece. I suddenly realized she was also Vesta Tilley.

A catalogue would be tedious. I have chosen rather to give some scenes fully enough for enjoyment—such as Sir Walter Scott's birthday celebrations on Windermere. I have never heard of a more completely successful party. Every one was brilliant or beautiful, no one fell in, no strawberry ice ruined any goffered petticoat. This is a topographical, not a literary or biographical essay. Where I have expanded somewhat, as on Ruskin at Brantwood, it is because I passionately saw things so and the expansion is not, I hope, inappropriate.

Its literary associations are, however, that aspect of its history in which the Lake District is unique. It is a mistake to think it had no history until the eighteenth century, but on the whole its rivers have run with sonnets rather than blood, and its most famous field commemorates not a battle but Dora's daffodils. "No record tells of lance opposed to lance", said Wordsworth in the Duddon Valley, and he said something in more places than Queen Elizabeth the First ever slept in.

It is clear from various remains that Stone Age man was at home in the Lake District and we may picture him living his primitive life high on the moors or along the middle heights which would be the only habitable parts, the tops being too hostile and the valley bottoms damp and unsuitable. For over 3,000 years man made very little head-way against nature, and the scenery on which Wordsworth gazed was the outcome of about 700 years of human effort shaping the landscape of pre-scientific days. Circles and cairns abound along the western edge of the district from Ennerdale Water to Black Combe, but comparatively little is known about them. The Keswick valley was well populated in late Neolithic times and there was an important colony in south Cumberland, centreing in Swinside. Such men hunted up Wastwater Screes, the Duddon Valley, Loughrigg and the wilder central dales, but they do not seem to have lived there. Men of the Bronze Age have left signs of having lived higher up the hill-sides than the Stone Age folk though they too avoided the heart of the real mountains. The foot of Ullswater, Sizergh Fell, Ambleside, western High Furness, and south Cumberland as well as the lower hills of the west were their chief habitation.

The Roman occupation was an interlude which did not leave much behind. Across the mountain called High Street runs an old track, and from there the road runs down towards the Roman fort at Brougham. This, and the fort at Ambleside, Hardknott Castle and Ravenglass represent the main Roman interest. I have expanded on it in the chapter on Eskdale. In A.D. 685 St. Cuthbert came to Carlisle. He found an abbey already there, and Anglian colonists. They had probably come from York over Stainmore. There were farm settlements sprinkled along the lower land of the coast, but except for St. Herebert, the hermit who lived on an island on Derwentwater, and a monastery at Dacre the Angles did not occupy the fell dales. The Britons survived sufficiently for some of them to be given to St. Cuthbert with Cartmel at the same time that he was given Carlisle. The dales would be too wooded and the fells would appeal only to shepherds of the hills, like the Norse. Nearly all early Lake District place names are Norse, except river names and one or two like Blencathra and Penruddock which prove the survival of Britons. Place names provide interesting clues to Lake District history. The name of some outstanding owner will be commemorated at the mouth of a valley, generally in a place ending in *by*. Higher up we find "booths" with the Gaelic name of some Irish or Scottish thrall whom the Norsemen brought with them to work dependent farms. Higher up again are summer shielings which grew into sheep farms, and at the heads of the valleys there are nearly always names which show that the wild forest was used for keeping pigs. In his *Lake District History* W. G. Collingwood plots many examples of such a sequence.

The south of England, in its precipitous way, became involved in decisive happenings in 1066. The north, with an even greater capacity for detachment then than now, was hardly affected until 1092 when William Rufus visited Cumberland. This sometimes kingly character was displaying his more ruffianly aspects at the time. He had refused to appoint a new Primate after Lanfranc's death and abrogated the revenues of Canterbury to himself. Fortunately, as the eleventh century closed the new lords were too busy consolidating the fat lowlands to trouble the inhabitants of

Silecroft, Cumberland ☛

the fells. Some of these must often have been in doubt as to whom they belonged and the visit of William Rufus was decisive in one respect. With the large army he brought he drove out Dolfin, the Scottish ruler of Carlisle, recovered the town, built the castle and included the whole of the Lake District in the English kingdom. Up to that date it had had bewildering uncertainty of ownership; from the Romans it passed to the kingdom of Strathclyde, was then under Anglian domination part of the great kingdom of Northumbria. The Vikings created confusion and a No Man's Land which at times became part of the Scottish kingdom. Rufus made it part of England. His brother, who succeeded him, Henry I, made the next great contribution when in 1122 he founded the bishopric of Carlisle. By the Norman castle should stand the Norman cathedral. From these stone symbols were to come the great system of the Middle Ages; the abbeys, monasteries and churches, the baronies and manors. Three houses of the Benedictine Order were founded in our district, the first and most important in 1127 by Stephen, count of Boulogne, lord of Lancaster, later King of England. This was Furness Abbey in the Vale of Nightshade. A second was at Calder, the third at Holm Cultram. Another land-owner in the Lake District was the great Yorkshire Cistercian Abbey of Fountains.

The mediaeval scene was set. The drama of the mediaeval synthesis that made one heaven and earth was under way. Barons and abbots cross the scene, and whilst in the periods of chaos and unrest the soldiers fought, the priests prayed. Even in these remote parts where the King's writ did not always run there was constant change in the ownership of land. Territorial ambitions, particularly over grazing grounds, clash; estates are bequeathed or inherited; chance takes a hand. When, for instance, "The Boy of Egremont" was drowned trying to jump the Strid at Bolton Abbey in Yorkshire his sister, Alice II de Rumeli, became heiress of Allerdale. Furness Abbey bought Borrowdale from her in 1209. Because the monks kept her receipts for the purchase we know that she was paid £156 13s. 4d. in all. The boundaries given in the agreement show how much of the mountain country was by then known and named. The same Alice disposed of land to Fountains and in 1211 the two abbeys made an agreement fixing their borders more exactly. Stonethwaite in Borrowdale was on the Fountains side, but when the dairy farm there became prosperous Furness tried to get it back. To and fro and up and up the dispute went from monks to abbots and Chapter-General and bishop and barons of the Exchequer till the king took the little vaccary of Stonethwaite into his own hands and Fountains got the pasturage from him for forty shillings. Our little Stonethwaite suddenly shines like a distant farm in a shaft of sunlight under that troubled sky.

A dark night in the Dark Ages must have been as dark in Borrowdale as anywhere could be. We must avoid the temptation spread by Ruskin or Morris or G. K. Chesterton to see the Middle Ages as like some rich tapestry—all stained glass windows and jolly guilds. The facts are even now only gradually emerging, but W. G. Collingwood has marshalled them in his history and C. M. L. Bouch has told more than the story of the diocese of Carlisle in his fascinating book, *Prelates and People of the Lake Counties*. The forests with their game and the needs of the sheep are predominant and recurring issues. Game, sheep, early industry, early capitalism, and other dominant themes were already given out, as by the different parts of an orchestra, before the Middle Ages had declined. Some we will take up as we come across them in covering the district. The not entirely dissimilar appearance of a Herdwick sheep on a fell-side can be as seminal an occasion for reflection as that of Wordsworth on Scafell Pike to the mind appropriately attuned, though it was not in fact so to Wordsworth, who showed a strange indifference to many agricultural matters amongst which he lived so much of his life. Pestilence and raiding that blew up at intervals to war took a proportion of their toll here as elsewhere. One national experience fell with peculiar harshness. The Reformation was indeed what Mr. Bouch calls it— a Northern tragedy. Henry VIII found the north poor and backward. The abbeys were its only wealth and civilizing influence, and them he robbed and destroyed. One must look to Furness Abbey for the explanation of so much that, though in our present terms it lies just outside the Lake

District, no opportunity to visit it should be missed. What remains of Fountains is more complete in itself and, if one can have a ranking list for such qualities, more beautiful and interesting. Furness has these qualities in abundance and must be, I imagine, one of the most extensive of such ruins. Anyone who goes to Barrow can easily visit it, but Barrow, though it is a fine modern town, has contrived to spring up in such an elaborately improbable spot that few people go there except on business which tends to exclude wandering round historic ruins. Yet given a couple of hours, the visitor can reconstruct from the remains of Furness, as convincingly as anywhere, the appearance and life of a great religious house. The red sandstone of which it is built has weathered and mellowed, and the arches spring beautifully against the green hill-sides and the hanging woods over the little river. Here, as elsewhere, smooth, shaven lawns make the perfect finish to a romantic ruin. They provide the only carpet for a building that is roofed with the sky. The slender arches soar to a breath-taking height. A kestrel, riding high above the nave, then gliding away through the empty eastern window, can emphasize the empyrean architecture. As usual, the monks chose a delightful sheltered spot in which to build. The hills that close in the valley and its stream have no doubt protected the ruin as they did the community that lived here. They have certainly made a perfect Shangri-la where even today one can re-capture the peaceful atmosphere despite certain changes.

The attendant was expatiating this summer to a party of mothers from Oldham on the advantages of the spot—protecting hills, trout stream, clear water for sanitation, etc., "They certainly knew how to choose", one of the women agreed. "And how sensible, too, to settle so near a railway."

Less as a poem than as a mnemonic by which to fix the circumstances of the abbey's foundation I strung the facts together thus:

> In the Vale of Deadly Nightshade
> In eleven twenty-seven,
> County Stephen of Bourgogne,
> Lord of Lancaster, who went to Heaven,
> God's anointed King of England

> Founded, so that all should bless
> His pious name and memory, this
> Cistercian Abbey in Furness.

Some absurd impulse moved me to recite it to the attendant when he told me various poems had been written about the place. He heard me in silence, then he said, "Well, there it is. You can always revise—or delete."

Speaking of the destruction of such abbeys as Fountains and Furness, Miss Rose Macaulay in her book *Pleasure of Ruins* described it as a crime for which there was not even the excuse of anti-clerical fury.

> What lives were led by individual monks matters little; like lives led elsewhere, they were, no doubt, mixed. What matters is the enshrining of an idea, the splendour and incomparable grace of the buildings, the libraries, the manuscripts, the fish-ponds, the vineyards, the grange barns, the ordered beauty of the religious services, the hospitality, the charity at the gates, the great bells that pealed over the countryside.

Gradually the raiding withdrew to the Border, but only ended when the union of the Crowns on the head of James Stuart brought peace and the opportunity to develop domestic architecture. We must leave the narrative to the historians who now know more of the lives of the Lake District people than did their contemporaries, though Queen Elizabeth had mining interests here, and Windermere char were becoming famous as Celia Fiennes and Camden bear witness. The district continued on the whole to be little known to the rest of the country. The Civil War and the Jacobite risings did not bring actual fights. The "statesmen", the typical yeomen on their own estates, had to find their own amusements—chiefly in their work or such sports as bull-baiting, fox-hunting, cock-fighting. Farming meant also spinning and they did not greatly miss the outside world. Then here and there the great world began to look in. Along the new turnpike roads they came in such numbers with their brand-new sensibilities that new inns had to be added to the old, to provide for all those who wanted to be in the new fashion of doting on scenery and "discovering" the lakes. "Curious travellers" indeed.

The most famous of them was, of course, the poet Gray who came in 1767 and 1769 and found particularly in Grasmere that "peace, rusticity and happy poverty in its neatest, most becoming attire" that attracted the romantic imagination more than the "rocks and cliffs of stupendous grandeur" though the romantic imagination enjoyed an occasional rather theatrical shudder. From then on each year saw its history, guide, "observations", excursion, laudatory ode or ramble till in 1788, according to Wilberforce, "the banks of the Thames are scarcely more public than those of Windermere". And that was only the beginning.

Before the literary and social invasion goes further we may note the disappearance from the changing scene of many of the freehold statesmen, absorbed into great estates or attracted to industrial towns. Many of the small holdings had been worked, and the farms built, by successive generations of one family and some of the oldest names now disappeared. At the same time the persistence of family names in the Lake counties is remarkable. Consider one—perhaps the oldest—for the interest it still has. For its early history I am indebted to Collingwood, who tells us that there was a man named Ealdred in the time of Edward the Confessor, English by name but canny by nature, for he managed to own considerable possessions and to keep on good terms with the authorities. His son Ketel had land in Kentdale and in Copeland about 1086 and married his son Orm to Gunilda, daughter of the great Earl Gospatrick who was descended "from all the famous old Kings of England and Scotland and was the chief man on both sides of the Border". His grandson, born about 1100, was named after him, and married a Norman, Egelina Engaine. Their son Thomas married a lady Grecia and acquired, probably with her, the lordship of Culwen in Kirkcudbright, whence the name Curwen, and he died about 1200. What am I coming to, and when? There is a time to whizz the film through, there is a time to peer at a single thread in the tapestry. The thread I have twisted out of its context in so rich a background links some of the discoveries with which this period of absorption in the subject of the Lake District has left me. How old some things are, how persistent and interwoven

Seascale, Cumberland, looking westward

are some of the threads, how strangely they renew themselves and how apparent it becomes that "the discovery of the Lakes" by the Romantics was in fact the discovery of themselves—a journey into the interior. I have taken this far backward glance at the origin of the Curwen family because like so many family names it runs through all the changing periods—Fletchers, Christians, Birketts, Wilkinsons, Wordsworths and others. Inter-related and often intermarried they form an integral society in themselves, their ramifications and real importance only to be properly understood by "one of us". The name Curwen presented itself for consideration here partly because towards the end of the eighteenth century, a time when he was much needed, appeared perhaps the greatest figure in local agricultural history. John Christian was born in 1756; in 1782 he married Isobella, daughter and sole heiress of Henry Curwen whose name he added to his own. He has been called "the father of Cumbrian farming", and as a result of extensive travel and wide experience he brought an enlightened mind to bear on the problems of local agriculture, introduced shorthorn cattle and realized the advisability of penning sheep on turnip land. Belle Island, which had formerly been called Curwen Island, was named after his wife, and he resided part of the year there until his death in 1828. His kinsman, Fletcher Christian, claims space for the remarkable story which can best be told when we reach Cockermouth. Here we may note that the pioneer agriculturist was succeeded in that role by Sir James Graham, of Netherby (1792 to 1861), whose energies were devoted mainly to improving systems of land drainage, a problem which would be vividly brought home to him on his own estates of Netherby on the low-lying land south of the Solway Firth. He is described in the Victoria County History as the most illustrious parliamentary figure that the county of Cumberland has ever produced. His work as an agriculturist was followed in Westmorland by Lord Lonsdale. Mention of Sir James Graham introduces yet another of the famous enduring names of this countryside that link up so many interesting aspects. His great-grandson, Sir Fergus Graham, continues the tradition of distinguished parliamentary service and devoted cultivation, particularly of the woodlands of the estate. The house has been contracted with great taste to suit the requirements of our own day, but you may still look out from the drawing-room windows across the Solway Firth to that Kirkcudbrightshire in which we have seen the origins of the Curwen family in the dim mists of time. For centuries the rule was "shoot at sight" when anyone was seen approaching across the flat marshlands from the Solway Firth. On the table in the hall you may still see where he wrote it, Sir Walter Scott's manuscript of *Young Lochinvar.*

It was, unfortunately, the effect of this necessary and enlightened interest in agriculture, together with such influences as that of the growth of spinning in factories, that broke up both the home industry and the freehold farms of so many of the yeomen statesmen of whom Wordsworth notes that between 1770 and 1820 their numbers were halved and the size of their holdings doubled.

Thus, with some institutions that had been long evolving now dropping away, replaced or discarded, and with new ideas and apprehensions growing up the nineteenth century rolled on. A high water mark of the Romantic period is 1834 when de Quincey published his *Reminiscences of the Lake Poets.* But before then, and indeed before 1800 when Coleridge settled there, Keswick had begun what is really the first chapter of residential and social life in the neighbourhood. It was less impregnated with literary associations than life nearer Windermere, and at the regattas, the first of which was held on Bassenthwaite lake in 1780 and afterwards for some years on Derwentwater, the subtle distinctions of the social hierarchy in English provincial life were well marked. Just as in the days of the three-deckers which carried our forebears of a few generations ago to be pioneers in New Zealand, bathing took place in the wastes of the Pacific Ocean at different times and from different places for the different classes, even so the arrangements on Derwentwater, particularly for skating, began to resemble those at English provincial "Assemblies", which to some extent survive even today, though we have to rely on the recollection of older people for the red velvet rope which divided even those who had managed to get there into those who were "us" and those who were not "us". Jane Austen made Elizabeth Bennett anticipate her visit to the lakes with romantic rapture. "What are men to rocks and mountains?" she cried, and though I shall forever regret that Elizabeth never reached nearer than Derbyshire I suspect that her creator would have been happier with the social material that now began to offer itself than with the ruder aspects of nature. Meanwhile we have, and must always be grateful for, W. G. Collingwood's *Lake District History*, which conducts us from the days of primitive man to the arrival of those residents of whom he says that: "Like the Vikings they first came on raids and then as immigrants." A hint, perhaps, of *nous autres*? In the social comedy of provincial life individuals may be geniuses but families constitute local society. In the chapter on Windermere something is said of the next stage in the invasion after the middle of the century which saw the settlement in the Lake District not of poets and writers and their distinguished friends but of what Mr. Bouch calls "ordinary men and women, who set up house in Keswick or Windermere in the same spirit as people in the south settle at Brighton or Bournemouth". I leave the speculative reader to ponder the validity of that.

Inevitably even the first tide of romantic enthusiasm set up its own reaction. Byron savaged one or two of the Lake poets and lesser men took a nip here and there. Charles Lamb charmingly deflated the scenery. Read him on how much better than Skiddaw as places to live in are the Strand and Fleet Street, and you'll love it. So delightful and amusing and safely enshrined in the culture gallery. But we whose love for the Lake District endures forget that like every other enthusiasm, whether for animals, speed, food, children or anything else, it provokes its own reaction.

"Not going there *again*?" said a friend incredulously. "I don't know how you can stand it—all rain and hikers with bare bony knees."

"I don't think you'll see many at the kind of expensive hotel you stay at," I said.

"No, but even there you'd always know where you were. You're sitting outside the hotel when a car draws up. The door opens, four great spaniels get out, then two women in brogues and tweeds. Now, if I'm getting out of a car, I expect a spaniel or even four spaniels to wait . . ."

They order these things better apparently, in Scotland. Then there is the townee's sort of irritation that Arnold Bennett, whose great gifts did not include the love of landscape, expressed in a letter to Hugh Walpole who had told him he had bought a "cottage" in the lakes. (Brackenburn is rather more than that.)

> Why the Lakes, my misguided friend? You will get wet through, and it is a hell of a way from London. Your touching sentimentality has led you to the Lakes. You wanted to get "into contact with Nature", didn't you? I bet you did, and of course the Lakes are the spiritual home of Nature. Never mind, my dear Hughie, I am entirely yours.

To which Hugh replied:

> Darling Arnold,
> *What* an insulting letter! But you've got nearly twenty years more cocksureness in your bundle than I have, so I'll say no more. I know that I am sentimental, romantic and slipshod—that's my "pattern in the carpet" . . . As to "going back to Nature", haven't I lived in the depths of Cornwall all my life? I went to the Lakes eight years running during my youth, so it's no new thing to me. And it *don't* rain all the time, and it's only seven hours from Keswick to London.

I am afraid my dear old friend showed his all too great capacity for being hurt, but I felt just the same when my favourite American writer on England, Ruth McKenney, in her best book *Here's England*—("the most beautiful, wonderful, exciting country in Europe" she describes it) in which she is so percipient where many are blind (about Durham for instance), wrote:

> Frankly we thought the Lake District dull. I am sure it is lovely holiday country for Englishmen who like walking tours, and mild scenery. Americans, however, have enough scenery in the homeland to do for three lifetimes. Borrowdale, Derwentwater, Rosthwaite, Seatoller, and the other scenic wonders look pretty pale compared to the Grand Canyon, the Rocky Mountains, or the Sierra Nevadas. They have some good

mountains in Switzerland, too. Why spend a fortune crossing the Atlantic, and wind up by a waterfall eleven feet high? I like scenery (fairly well), but if you are going in for scenery, it might as well be first-class. For instance, the trip up to the saddle of the Jungfrau is *scenery*.

The Lake District is, I admit it, hallowed and all that. Tourists file in by the left-hand queue and exit (amid the pushing and shoving of the Youth Hostel set) by the right, through Wordsworth's vine-covered cottage. Shelley brought one of the Mrs. Shelleys here on their wedding trip—X marks the spot. One warning: The Lakes are crowded in the top of the summer season. Probably you can find a hotel, if you should arrive unheralded, but most tourists are "booked" for the Lakes through travel agencies. Travel Bureaux are apt to lay on heavily when describing the glories of Borrowdale. Food in the Lake District is strictly Tourist Grade, with plenty of that good old Windsor-Stratford cooking.

What a Scrooge I sound! And the Lake District is so quaint too! . . . If you would rather not have chin-bearded ancients press four-leaf clovers upon you, you will do better to concentrate on Newstead Abbey and the Derbyshire valley of the Wye—for this is *really* England, industrial and glorious.

Ah well! *De gustibus*, I always say, *non disputandum*.

A dash of bitters improves many a sweet draught. Moreover—

> God gives all men all earth to love,
> But, since man's heart is small,
> Ordains for each one spot shall prove
> Beloved over all.

Those of us for whom that means the Lake District (some "spot"!) can never feel that it lacks appreciation. Indeed, dare we whisper it? We are glad of anything that will deflect visitors; but that may be a culpable attitude as we move into the era when the whole area may be in process of becoming a national park. Many societies prepared the way but with the growth of the National Trust we really begin to enter into our heritage.

The Lake District and the National Trust by B. L. Thompson (Titus Wilson & Son), a longer book than this, tells the story of this aspect of the Lake District in a fascinating way. Although Mr. Bruce Thompson approaches the subject

primarily from the point of view of the National Trust with
which he is so loyally identified, his book is full of interesting
lore not to be found elsewhere on many different aspects,
especially of flora and fauna. This, and his sensitive appreciation of the scenery make this one of the best books on the
Lake District. Of the three people always considered the
founders of the National Trust one, Canon H. D. Rawnsley,
was of course famous as a Lake District lover and it was
appropriate that at least one person from the district should
be in at the birth. The other two, Miss Octavia Hill, the
famous housing reformer whose home was in Kent, and
Sir Robert Hunter, the solicitor to the Post Office who lived
in Surrey, were both very frequent visitors to the district.
All three were remarkable people, strongly idealistic and a
very effective team. We are all indebted to those who have
built on their foundations. The story of the various fights
to save well-known beauty spots and of the generosity of the
public-spirited donors who have constantly added to the
properties owned by the Trust is excellently told by Mr.
Thompson. I cannot do better than direct the reader to his
book.

I conclude these rather rambling observations with a word
or two about the plan of this book. It is closely related to
the fact that everyone knows that the lakes and valleys
roughly radiate from the central massif. To revert for a
moment to the exiguous sketch of the geology that we have
left behind we may note that in the long-lost centuries between
the emergence of the dry land for the last time and the
appearance of Wordsworth on Scafell Pike tremendous
agencies were at work. A great dome of rock with its greatest
height on a line from Scafell to Helvellyn sloped downwards
gradually to north and south. To the north was a secondary
summit which we call Skiddaw. The very shape of this
formation would cause the waters of great rainstorms to
wash away from it as the seven great valleys still do. Then
came the Ice Age and the next stage of Nature's cosmic
sculpture. I revert thus briefly in order to help myself out
with the old image of the spokes of a wheel—or would it be
more contemporary to think of the sections of a dart-board?

Anyhow, the end result is that on a short holiday unless you are touring you tend to find yourself staying in one of these sections, and in this book I have described them one after the other in a clockwise motion. In each section my interest has been in the scenery and story, the geology where it was usefully apparent, the buildings, the literary associations, and the progress of the National Trust. Those are recurring interests wherever one finds oneself. There are, however, many general aspects of the Lake District on every one of which volumes larger than this have been written, and I have taken the opportunity to deal with these as best I could where they arose most naturally. For instance, in Eskdale, apart from everything else to be described, the Romans provided the topic for conversation "that night at the Inn". Those words are generally the sign that some subject which specifically arises in that section is, so far as possible, polished off as a whole whilst there is time and opportunity. In the chapter on Coniston I have generalized about farm-houses, in that on Wasdale about climbers, and elsewhere on sheep, tourists, houses, sport, and so on.

All is inadequate. Reader, you must piece out my imperfections with your own thoughts and experiences. May you find much happiness in doing so.

CHAPTER II

Windermere

A VIEWPOINT is as good a place to begin as any. Just above Windermere station, from the terrace of what it still seems strange to some of us not to think of as Riggs Hotel, there is a view, immediate and remarkable, in a way more characteristic of Continental holiday resorts than of English. At Lucerne, at Montreux, at Lugano, at so many well-organized places, the view is commanded as an amenity by the hotel. This is so seldom the case with us that one can understand an Englishman confronted with this view murmuring absent-mindedly: "Ah, if only we had scenery like this in our country."

Orrest Head, an easily accessible point above the hotel, adds sufficient vantage to earn one of Mr. Baddeley's superlatives. It is "the finest extensive viewpoint in the Lake District, and, perhaps, the finest in Great Britain"; an inspiring start. There will be other memorable viewpoints, but if our ruminations here are indulgently prolonged it must be because they have to generalize to some degree for the many other points from which, however tempted, we shall be forever hurrying on. But first, to be specific.

The incomparable lake, the river-lake as it now seems, so long and winding, lies at your feet, with its islands, bays, creeks, ferries, yachts and winding wooded shore—England's greatest mere, Winander. Behind rise the fells and the mountains, a great cross-section of the giants who await us. Nothing is more irritating than the companion who cannot enjoy a glimpse of the most distant mountain unless he can be sure of its name. On the other hand the most impressionistic traveller could hardly resist the way in which, as the curtain rises on so spectacular a

scene, the panorama of peaks present themselves for identi-
fication.

The first obvious mountain above the south end of the lake
is Coniston Old Man with Dow Crag and Walna Scar to the
left and a glimpse of Black Combe. To the right of the Old
Man you will see Wetherlam rounded and more prominent,
with the sharp spur of Carrs behind. So far we are in
Lancashire but to the north of Wetherlam a slight dip indi-
dates Wrynose Gap and there above the upper reaches of
the Duddon valley, the counties of Lancashire, Westmorland
and Cumberland run "towards each other and the sky", and
meet almost on the summit of the fells. Then come Cold Pike,
and Pike o' Blisco with flat tops, and Crinkle Crags, whose
name alone almost identifies their crest. The great landmark
of Bow Fell, with Scafell Pike nearly three miles farther
back to the left, mark the remote heart of the Lake District.
What looks like the northern spur of Bow Fell is Great End,
the northern bastion of this central massif. Just beneath it
is the dip of Esk Hause and Allen Crags whence, as we shall
find in later explorations, Derwent and Esk rise and the
various streams that feed the head of Wasdale. How
different a scene Great Gable, of which from here we get a
glimpse just to the left of Langdale Pikes, looks down on in
Wasdale from the one before us. Nearer to us is the unmis-
takeable double hump of the Langdale Pikes. Across the
dip of Great Langdale is the steep ridge of Pavey Ark. Then
comes a long straight line, with one protuberance, Sergeant
Man, to the point at which the road below where we are
standing clearly goes over the sky-line. Loughrigg Fell is
the near eminence, Helm Crag has a distinctive outline, and
to the right rise Nab Scar and Fairfield all but hidden from
here by Wansfell Pike. Then come noticeably Red Screes,
and after Troutbeck, High Street, Froswick, and Ill Bell,
with sharp summits, Harter Fell, and away in the south-east
the unmistakable long snout-nosed summit of Ingleborough.
To the right stretch the sands and waters of Morecambe
Bay.

It is an array of peaks that cannot be lived up to; but
beneath us are the many houses of those who have found
that it can be lived in front of—and despite playing old

Harry with our prepositions in a way that would distress him, we may invoke Walter Pater in defence of suburbs (and Windermere has become comfortably ideal with its homes and gardens): "Nowhere are things more apt to respond to the brighter weather, nowhere is there so much difference between rain and sunshine, nowhere do the clouds roll together more grandly; those quaint suburban pastorals gathering an unmistakable quality of grandeur from the background", in this case of mountains and lake. The case for man-made scenery versus that of Nature unaided is not likely to be won in the Lake District, the true answer being probably that the ideal is the co-operation that was briefly achieved here in the eighteenth century, but nobody will deny that a garden is immensely improved by a background of water and fells, as is multifariously shown in Windermere. A lawn from which the Langdale Pikes appear to rise is like no other lawn. I do not find residential Windermere devoid of charm. Much of it was built at a period, beginning just over a century ago, for which architecturally the word "unfortunate" seems to be reserved. We have seen in recent years some striking re-assessments of its products. Hardly ten years separates the two following assessments:

But the houses of the nineteenth-century influx of gentry and near-gentry are loathly. If a Swiss chalet and a London suburban villa committed miscegenation and the off-spring was made of a peculiar dark, unyielding, slaty stone, and inherited three storeys and at least two gables from one parent and horrible fretted wood gable-decorations from the other, there you would have the typical Lakeland lodging-house.

Everything is wrong with it. Its stones are not hewn big and square, but thin and regular; the colour of this new slate has no mellowness; the roofs are harsh and cold—and why gables? And the squirly bits of wooden edging here and there look merely meretricious. Bow-windows abound; about seventy-five per cent are adorned with bamboo tables and aspidistras. Whole streets of Windermere, Ambleside, Keswick—and a large part of Grasmere—could be translated to Bayswater or Muswell Hill, and would look perfectly at home.

We are going to depart from the town of Windermere without another look, and make for Ambleside.

Thus, emphatically, Miss Doreen Wallace; and thus Mr. Norman Nicholson:

Windermere is a strange town in that it owes its existence almost entirely to the visitors. It is not really a native town at all, but it manages to achieve an unexpected dignity, with its slate boarding-houses and bay-windows. Here, the nearness of the limestone has led the builders to use rough blocks of it for window-sills instead of sandstone. So we have houses in two shades of grey, or rather gray, for one vowel seems darker to me than the other.

This is an interesting tribute from the poet of our day who, more than any other, has found inspiration in the rocks and stones of the earth before the coming of man. The present subject clearly awaits Mr. John Betjeman, the poet who has been most concerned with what man has done with the stones, and that latterly. So far as I can recall, that topographical genius has only taken one tantalizing nibble at our area.

Spirit of Grasmere, bells of Ambleside,
Sing you and ring you, water bells, for me;
Yon water-colour waterfalls may froth.
Long hiking holidays will yet provide
Long stony lanes and back at six to tea
And Heinz's ketchup on the tablecloth.

One building quite worthy of interest Windermere can offer: the Parish Church near the pier at Bowness. It is fifteenth century, much restored in parts, but with a fascinating east window. This is really a unique combination of several old windows, in the Late Perpendicular period (1430–80) but much of the glass which came from Cartmel Priory is older, some dating back to 1260. The church contains many interesting memorials at one of which at least, a handsome carved oak prayer desk, one gazes with respect, gratitude and awe. It commemorates the great Baddeley himself—him of the Thorough Guides. The squat red volume on the Lake District has accompanied us for so many years to mountain tops and far places, has been drenched, become dog-eared, but remains the essential, indispensable companion. A personality, omniscient, autocratic, didactic, was

reflected in those factual pages, one who did not suffer fools
gladly, an austere character, not indulgent to "potterers"
and the like. After covering all the peaks he throws in a
chapter of odd "days on the fells" that makes the limbs
ache to read, and follows it with one on "descents from the
fells" in emergencies and by routes that make the timid
reader constantly perspire. A failure in this world is a
casualty and since boyhood I have in nightmares fallen to
the foot of terrible precipices and entered heaven to be
greeted by a reproachful Baddeley demonstrating the
difference between true and magnetic north or between a
path and a county boundary.

His work, like that of Mrs. Beeton, reflects in its successive
editions the changing social scene, though his later editors
have preserved more than hers the individual tone of the
author's voice. The earliest edition I have is the sixth, of
1891. One reads with pleasure that Riggs' four-horse coaches
have a county-wide reputation, that regular stage-coaches
ply. Private conveyances are a shilling a mile, one and six-
pence pair-horse, driver threepence, carriage and pair twenty
to thirty shillings a day, plus driver and road expenses. Not
cheap. Especially as at the hotel, according to our mentor,
"the hungry tourist fails to be satisfied with his one 'portion'
and, as often as not goes in for 'Benjamin's mess', with the
result of having his bill doubled". I delight in assembling a tiny
anthology of his pronounced and therefore for me definitive
ultimates or superlatives. For example do you know which
is the finest waterfall scene in the district?—Stanley Ghyll
in Eskdale; the handsomest view in England?—of Windermere and beyond from the Troutbeck road to Patterdale;
the steepest approach to any railway station in the country?
—Dent; the most picturesquely situated milestone?—the
fifth from Penrith on the road from Alston; the finest viewpoint in the Lake District and perhaps the finest in Great
Britain?—where we came in, Orrest Head.

He is rightly commemorated, for no writer on the Lake
District has been of more practical assistance to its lovers
for three-quarters of a century. His wife's memorial to him
is the one we saw in the church (one notes with respect that
his Christian name was, and one feels appropriately,

Mountford). The clock tower half-way between Windermere Station and Bowness Pier is also a memorial. His remains lie in the cemetery past the pier at the far end of the Glebe, with its miniature golf-course. It seems, remembering his nightmare domination of one, a singularly sheltered, almost domestic haven. And it is bracing to be able to add the fortifying detail (see Baddeley current, twentieth edition, and, of course, long long, *eheu, posthumous, eheu!*): "The tombstones were conveyed with great labour from the summit of Scafell Pike." *Labuntur anni* appropriately remembered!

The residents who have followed Mr. Baddeley's final example have shown a first sign of grace in seeking to live here, and they make it their business in most cases to preserve the amenities. They are the appreciative denizens. The indigenous country folk whom we shall meet in other parts are pre-occupied with many things before the picturesque. What of the visitors—not such as our dear selves but the daily trippers? In an account of a district so remarkably picturesque it would be absurd to speak only of the correspondingly picturesque and early visitors like Celia Fiennes and Gray without examining what came in their train. Such abundance of good awaits us it exacts a full look at the worst. To Windermere by rail and road come the holiday-makers, more particularly the day trippers. The lake accepts them with as little discrimination as the sea in Auden's poem which can serve as an admirable description of Bowness in the season.

> August for the people and their favourite island.
> Daily the steamers sidle up to meet
> The effusive welcome of the pier, and soon
> The luxuriant life of the steep stone valleys,
> The sallow oval faces of the city
> Begot in passion or good-natured habit,
> Are caught by waiting coaches, or laid bare
> Beside the undiscriminating sea.
>
> Lulled by the light they live their dreams of freedom;
> May climb the old road twisting to the moors,
> Play leap frog, enter cafés, wear
> The tigerish blazer and the dove-like shoe.

The yachts upon the little lake are theirs,
The gulls ask for them, and to them the band
Makes its tremendous statements; they control
The complicated apparatus of amusement.

The coaches are the evolved equivalent in our day of the
ones in which we picture Parson Woodforde travelling in the
eighteenth century and after him Becky Sharp, and David
Copperfield and Tom Brown whose journeys were marked by
such enjoyable gigantic repasts. The railways drove the
coaches off the roads for a time but they long ago re-estab-
lished themselves. Figures of all kinds will appear in the
landscape in which we are interested. The account would
be misleading that did not include the impact of the coaches
so characteristic of our day.

Some men a forward motion love,
But I, by backward steps, would move . . .

Nevertheless I rode in a coach this summer. I joined it at
Bowness, where the shores of Windermere had been transformed by excursionists to such a replica of Blackpool that
the old backcloth of Helvellyn and Dollywaggon Pike seemed
culpably old-fashioned. We bowled across the poor scarred
face of England; and as we bowled we sang. I was reminded
of something in Trevelyan about the Elizabethans singing
their madrigals in the lanes and roads down which their
descendants pass in noisy silence, and I recollected something in Pepys about his boat passing another on the Thames
and each boat took up the tune that floated across the water
from the other until they were out of hearing. In our coach
we sang a song in which, after brief verses, there recurred
the refrain, "Bobbing up and down". This we demonstrated.
They were singing it, I noticed, in nearly every coach that
went by.

We must not romanticize the past. I remember that David
Copperfield was very uncomfortable in his coach, crushed
between the men on either side who nearly smothered him
when they fell asleep, harassed by the lady in front wrapped
up like a haystack who lodged her basket under his short
legs. And though in my coach we did not get what Tom

Brown got to eat we called at the equivalent of a coaching inn. It catered specially for our kind. Beer flowed for hundreds of patrons and among the uproar impromptu entertainers sang or danced—one woman in a straw skirt, another in practically no skirt at all. At intervals as many as another hundred men and women would surge in as more coaches drew up and at last the earlier customers were driven on to the roadside, into the air and the Sunday evening sunset.

Behind them, amongst the lonely hills, the silence waited.

Very different are those who have without impropriety revived an old word, the hikers. They tend to pass through Windermere assembling in large flocks at Ambleside, a better centre for their exertions. There, booted and hob-nailed, laden like pack-camels, with bare knees and legs, maps, sandwiches, they fill the post-card shops. It takes fewer of them than of less cumbered people to fill the shop, but you may turn them on their axis by means of their packs and manœuvre for position. Away from the assembly centres they will be encountered in the remotest spots, in small groups, pairs, or singly, agile as mountain gazelles, hardy as camels. They walk because they love the district and have entered into their heritage. They experience physical exhilarations unknown to motorists and always and only provided that they leave no litter many of them belong to what Mr. Symonds, austerest of writers for the real walkers, refers to as "the brotherhood". The consideration of them recalls us to our proper pre-occupation.

We may lift up our eyes to the hills but the characteristic pleasures of Windermere are those of the lake, the winding shore and the islands, the water itself, with the fish beneath, the birds and boats upon it and the clouds that float above and are reflected in it. The administrative arrangements are of a pleasing complexity. The west shore and the east shore half-way up are in Lancashire. The rest of the shore is in Westmorland, as is the entire permanent lake floor. As a Lancashire resident you may keep a boat on your shore. If you build a boat-house that projects into the water it will rest on Westmorland. The whole lake is within the parish of the Vicar of Windermere, who has the right to a pleasure boat and a tithe of the fish caught. The lawyers have had their fun in successive centuries with those whom these arrangements have brought into collision ever since the monks of Furness and the holders of the barony of Kendal pioneered in local government and self-seeking.

The passage of time seems to blunt the distinction between heroes and villains, however strong the passions that played round them in their day. All tend to survive mainly for their characteristic manifestations of vitality. Windermere claims a high percentage of picturesque figures who still catch the imagination. Two at least may be commemorated before we leave Orrest Head.

The grounds along the foot of the hill itself were laid out as part of the estate known as Elleray which, at the beginning of the last century, took the fancy of a young man, John Wilson, when he was still an undergraduate at Oxford. At the age of twenty-two, having inherited £40,000 he bought the estate and became a titanic figure in the landscape. Six feet high, broad-shouldered, athletic, vigorous, fanciful, one catches glimpses of him, collarless and clothing otherwise improvised, fishing, hunting, striding forty miles over the hills, riding his famous pony Colonsay, and with two friends, each armed with a spear, even chasing a bull across the uplands by moonlight.

Dancing, wrestling, boxing, cock-fighting, drinking hard, sailing so many boats he was dubbed "Lord High Admiral of Windermere", he seemed indeed to have, as somebody said, the roistering vigour of an ancient Viking, or the necessary qualifications of a hero for Ouida who would certainly have delighted in the additional recorded fact that a fledgling sparrow that took refuge in his study was fed and cared for and became so tame that it remained a denizen of the same room for at least eleven years. (". . . with his girlish hands that Duchesses envied he had grappled lions in the jungle . . ." It is almost of a piece.) A poet (a Newdigate prize-winner), he was a centre of the literary life of the district and was himself later under the name of Christopher North famous and widely read.

All this tumultuous energy was harnessed when through a defaulting trustee his fortune was lost. Although he retained Elleray he returned to Edinburgh. There he became a dominant figure on the staff of the newly-formed *Blackwood's Magazine*. He also became Professor of Moral Philosophy, acquiring the qualifications after securing the job. He also took Sir Walter Scott's advice to "forswear sack, purge and live cleanly like a gentleman".

Scott and his daughter stayed at Elleray, and in 1825 in honour of Scott's fifty-fourth birthday Wilson arranged the celebrations. Lockhart's account deserves more than the usual snippets of quotation, the scene so shines under the sun and moon of a vanished era.

Mr. Bolton's seat, Storrs to which Canning had invited Scott, is situated a couple of miles lower down on the same Lake; and thither Mr. Wilson conducted him next day. A large company had been assembled there in honour of the Minister—it included already Mr. Wordsworth. It has not, I suppose, often happened to a plain English merchant, wholly the architect of his own fortunes, to entertain at one time a party embracing so many illustrious names. He was proud of his guests; they respected him, and honoured and loved each other; and it would have been difficult to say which star in the constellation shone with the brightest or the softest light. There was "high discourse", intermingled with as gay flashings of courtly wit as ever Canning displayed; and a plentiful allowance, on all sides, of those airy transient pleasantries, in which the fancy of poets, however wise and grave, delights to run riot when they are sure not to be misunderstood. There were beautiful and accomplished women to adorn and enjoy this circle. The weather was as Elysian as the scenery. There were brilliant cavalcades through the woods in the mornings, and delicious boatings on the Lake by moonlight; and the last day "the Admiral of the Lake" presided over one of the most splendid regattas that ever enlivened Windermere. Perhaps there were not fewer than fifty barges following in the Professor's radiant procession when it paused at the point of Storrs to admit into the place of honour the vessel that carried kind and happy Mr. Bolton and his guests. The bards of the Lakes led the cheers that hailed Scott and Canning; and music and sunshine, flags, streamers, and gay dresses, the merry hum of voices, and the rapid splashing of innumerable oars, made up a dazzling mixture of sensations as the flotilla wound its way among the richly-foliaged islands, and along bays and promontories peopled with enthusiastic spectators.

His circle of friends at Windermere included Wordsworth,
de Quincey, the Coleridges, Southey and old Bishop Watson
of Calgarth, the estate a very little way from Elleray nearer
Ambleside and which you may cross in the descent from
Orrest Head. The others in this circle of friends are figures
in the pantheon of the Lake District, if not specifically of
Windermere. That Bishop Watson should have a place in
the story at all is remarkable, one may even think scandalous.
His life should have been part of the story of Llandaff, but
he was one of the most accomplished absentees in history.
Every Welshman, it is said, knows of him but few Welshmen,
in his lifetime, ever set eyes on him. He is a well-known
figure, but his story is told by nobody so well I think as
by A. G. Bradley, who, in the old Highways and Byways
volume, writes of him with a sort of round-eyed incredulity
which, of course, we all share if we consider in our over-taxed
days a village schoolmaster's son who managed to enjoy
from various sources an income of £5,000 by doing nothing
at all.

He was born in Westmorland, did well at Cambridge in
mathematics, and early in life was appointed Professor of
Chemistry, of which he knew nothing, but like Professor
Wilson quickly picked up what he lacked. He did not bother
to show the same assiduity in the matter of Divinity, of
which he managed to secure for himself the professorship at
the age of thirty-five. In that faculty he concentrated on
raising the stipend to £1,000 a year, of which he paid £300
to a substitute. "His next triumph", says Bradley, "was the
bishopric of Llandaff, and this achieved he went to live in
Westmorland by way of being handy to his duties in South
Wales, bought Calgarth, married a county lady, and settled
down to the pursuits of a country gentleman." There was
some indignation in Glamorgan that he was never promoted.
We have the bishop's word for it that it was because the
squires felt the Whig Government had been unappreciative
of his support, but there must have been an unsmiling
complacency about a man who in his position could then
issue a circular mandate to his clergy on the evil of absentee-
ism. One had begun to look for a genius, but unlike Becky
Sharp, who practised the gentle kindred art of how to live

on nothing a year, he was according to his neighbour, de Quincey, quite uninteresting as a man, pompous and heavy-minded.

> All his public, all his professional duties [says de Quincey] he systematically neglected. He was a lord in Parliament and for many a year he never attended the place; he was a bishop and he scarcely knew any part of his diocese by sight, living three hundred miles away from it; he was a professor of divinity holding the richest professorship in Europe—the weightiest for its functions in England—drawing by his own admission one thousand per annum from its endowments, and for thirty years he never read a lecture or performed a public exercise!

In spite of all this, he came, amazingly, within an ace of being Archbishop of York! Lady Holland told Wordsworth that Fox and Grenville had quite decided to offer him that post which promised soon to be vacant. But as in some novel Trollope might have devised, the Archbishop just outlived the Administration!

Yet how difficult it is to arrive at a just assessment is shown by the way the same facts are stated in a different tone by the Reverend Norman Sykes in his scholarly work *Church and State in England in the XVIIIth Century* (Cambridge University Press, 1934) where he writes:

> Since the entire record of Watson's life refutes at once any whisper of insincerity of speech or innate lethargy of disposition, the reason for his complacent acquiescence in his own protracted non-residence in his diocese and preoccupation with the agricultural pursuits of his home at Windermere must be sought elsewhere than in suggestions of deliberate infidelity to duty or hypocrisy in undertaking the office and work of a bishop. The explanation is to be found in the circumstances of the poverty of his see and its lack of episcopal residence on the one part, and in the disappointment engendered by his long neglect at the hands of ministers of state on the other part, as testified by their failure to offer the expected translation. To the importance of both conditions his autobiographical narrative bears the fullest testimony.

The banks of Windermere are indebted to him for extensive tree-planting and the story of The Cock, an old tavern he

Mardale, looking west-north-west ☛

bought in Ambleside. The landlord thought to exploit this and changed the name to The Bishop. A rival promptly took up the discarded name and prospered. In some alarm the first landlord painted under the portrait of the bishop: "This is the Old Cock."

The lake itself seems designed for pleasure and recreation in a manner which would be alien to, say, Wastwater. The steamers that ply from end to end, the launches with their parties, the motor-boats, and yachts all offer vantage points and still generally leave solitude enough for the small boat that seeks it, and the beauties of the winding coast. The chief of the charming wooded islands is called Belle Isle. It may be that the Romans were there. From about 1250 when it was known as Longholme it was the seat of the lord of the manor of Windermere. It became the property and residence of the ancient Westmorland family of Philipson who had a tower here which, in the Civil War, was besieged by Col. Briggs, a Kendal magistrate and a Cromwellian officer. It was pulled down by Mr. English, who built the "Tea-caddy" in 1774. The island then passed into the ownership of the Curwen family and became Curwen's Island; and it is from Isobella Curwen that its present name derives. She was a cousin of Fletcher Christian whose story can be more appropriately recalled at Cockermouth.

The shore of the lake from Bowness to Newby Bridge is best explored from the lake rather than from the wood-shrouded road, but Gummer's How near the bottom on the east side and Finsthwaite Tower on the opposite side yield splendid views. The upper reach of Windermere from Bowness to Low Wood and Ambleside is inexhaustibly beautiful. The absentee bishop's house is now the Ethel Hedley Orthopaedic Hospital, and on the other side of the lake, at Wray Castle, a modern building in a setting of great natural beauty and a National Trust property, is the head-quarters of the Freshwater Biological Association. To increase the numbers of trout and of the char, for which Windermere was famous when Celia Fiennes was here in 1698, the Association trap tons of pike and perch each September.

There is delightful unspoilt country south of Windermere

in the Winster valley. Kentmere, Long Sleddale and Mardale, all easily explored from here, yield beauty and interest unknown to many who claim to know the Lake District. Those who get as far as Haweswater will be rewarded by the noble austerity of its setting of which its conversion into a reservoir for Manchester has not robbed it. The original Dun Bull, now submerged, was a famous old hostelry. For generations shepherds met there every November and when the day had been consumed with sheep affairs the evening would bring on a tatie-pot supper and a dance. Far below the level of the present hotel the old place, part farm, part inn, lay cradled in the semicircle of mountains at the head of the lake. It was of the type of Lakeland hostelry, now almost vanished, that flourished in the days of the pack-horse trains for which it was the first inhabited house where Nan Bield Pass comes into Mardale from Kentmere, Staveley, and Kendal. On the way to Penrith on the Border it was a welcome place of refreshment for the pack animals and their drivers, the batemen who are perpetuated in a local surname.

When the valley was submerged the parish of Mardale practically ceased to exist. The remaining fragments were attached to Bampton. The fabric of the early eighteenth-century church was removed and the bodies in the graveyard were transferred to Bampton. Do the tall yew trees that guarded them for so long still stand erect beneath the shadowy waters? Among the submerged graves was that of the last direct male heir, who died towards the close of the nineteenth century, of the Holme family, hereditary monarchs of what was long known, tiny as it was, as the kingdom of Mardale. The first recorded member of the family to come here was Hugh Holme who, fleeing from the wrath of King John early in the thirteenth century, was given sanctuary by the owner of the dale whose land he ultimately purchased. His descendants were called Kings of Mardale.

Gate Scarth Pass leads out of Mardale under the crags of Harter Fell to Long Sleddale which leads down to Kendal and lies perhaps beyond our immediate concern but we may note, whilst on the subject of local dishes, that in "Wet" Sleddale, as it is also called, they make "yarb" (herb) puddings in the spring from Bistort—a most unlikely plant locally called Easter Ledges or Easterman Giants—of baffling etymology. It is possibly a relict of the need for an anti-scorbutic after a winter without vitamin C.

Troutbeck and Kentmere are, on the other hand, undoubtedly integral to the Lake District. The road from Windermere to Troutbeck is the beginning of the most picturesque way to Patterdale, but we will reserve Ullswater which itself is best seen from the opposite end and approach it from Keswick. The climb up to Troutbeck reveals with each step beautiful backward views and indeed at the Borrans at the top of the rise is "perhaps the most beautifully situated house in Britain". The foreground is all richly wooded luxuriance and gentle lake scenery merging into the impressive background of fells at the top of the valley. In the picturesque village of Troutbeck beside the National Trust possession of Town End Farm is a famous inn, the Mortal Man, where a modern signboard has replaced the original one which carried the legend:

> O mortal man that liv'st on bread,
> How comes thy nose to be so red?
> Thou silly ass, that look'st so pale,
> It comes of Sally Birkett's ale.

The valley is full of interest but we must leave it by the Garburn Pass to see Kentmere Vale. The head of upper Kentmere is striking and Troutbeck as it drops behind seems at every step to lie deeper under the slopes of Ill Bell and Wansfell with High Street, Caudale Moor and Red Screes dominating the upper valley. Baddeley gives the strange history of Kentmere:

Many people, on entering this valley, will ask, why Kent*mere*? Except for a modern reservoir at the head of the valley, there is no mere at all. Look down the valley, however. More than a century ago the valley possessed a lake a mile long, the delight of the fisherman, and an adornment to a scene which, with it, was beautiful—without it, is bare and desolate. However, "Hodge" set to work, and at vast trouble and expense scooped out a deep channel at the foot of the lake. The waters rushed down it, and lo! in place of a lake, a marsh! Huge heaps of slate and soil at the south end of the morass and modern diatomite works are a further disfigurement.

This is the country of Mrs. Humphry Ward's *Robert Ellesmere*, and in Troutbeck one who had abandoned the role of writer and the name of Beatrix Potter and identified herself with the enterprising farmer Mrs. Heelis, might have been seen leaning against a sheltering rock scanning the hillside of Troutbeck valley and studying the Herdwick sheep in which she had deeply interested herself. All over the district we shall encounter these characteristic creatures of the fells, small, with grey faces, hardy and active. They yield excellent meat. There have been many arguments about their origin. The least likely perhaps is the tradition of a stranded ship from the Spanish Armada. Their forebears may have been brought over by the Vikings in the tenth century or they may have an even earlier ancestry in the flocks the Britons must have had here.

The sheep and dairy farming which we see here are characteristic of agriculture throughout the Lake District. Wordsworth's "green corn rustling" and the Rye-dale in the name Rydal echo the period when because of its isolation the district had to try to be self-supporting. Today, apart from the cattle on the rather limited pasture land in the meadow valleys, sheep farming is the main agricultural activity.

The fell farmer who has level fields is lucky; too often his cattle have to eke a living out of the intakes stretching high on to the fell-sides. Bracken, weather and gradient are the enemies. Bracken would quickly swallow most of the fell farmer's land if he did not keep it in check, a job which itself makes the whole operation of a lowland farm seem easy. But the intakes are clean and their bright green is laid like broad cloths on the mountain-sides proclaiming man's victory over the wilderness.

The fell farmer may still have to fill in his forms by the light of an oil lamp, and his wife cook on a coal range, but he can still—and often does—have an excellent herd of cattle, which fetches top prices at the local auction mart. His milk cheques and wool clips pay the bills, but there's a bit of his forefathers still in the farmer who raises beef cattle second to none, and sheep which can cut down to the most succulent of mutton.

The men who made the Lake District farms were giants among men, their descendants remain giants among farmers. They are not, perhaps, so well off as their lowland colleagues, but they have about them an air of well-being, not brought about by the possession of worldly goods, but by the holding in their hands, and theirs alone, of the power to tame the wild lands. Their produce and their income proclaim them as "small farmers", but their stock roams over far-stretching ranges. After lambing, their sheep—and other breeds are raised besides Herdwicks—are turned out on to the fells. To the casual visitor they seem abandoned and few, but when the "round-up" is under way, when the sheep are brought down for market or to be put into winter quarters on lower ground, the scattered grey shapes gradually collect into a dull silver torrent which is eased down the fell-sides by patient men and dogs.

A hard winter with heavy snow can mean catastrophe for the fell farmer. His sheep—or those of them that are left on the fells—will huddle together in a sheltered place and allow the snow to cover them completely. They can keep alive for just so long, so the shepherd and his dogs go out to search for and rescue them. The dogs smell out the snow-bound sheep, the shepherd probably helped by his wife and children—digs them out. Sometimes they are too late, sometimes the sheep are never found and there is food for the buzzards, ravens and carrion crows when the thaw sets in, and a dead loss for the farmer.

Coniston

ARMING and farm-houses are predominant themes of
all the countryside on both sides of Windermere. If we
take the ferry and cross the lake we shall find ourselves
on the pleasant way to Hawkshead, but before we get there
we shall reach the twin villages of Sawrey, Near and Far by
less than a mile. The point of reference recalls Hawkshead
in the days when it took precedence of Windermere as a
centre. To the north stretch Claife Heights. To the south is
all the green, fertile, gentle countryside that lies between
Windermere and Coniston. It was at Sawrey that Beatrix
Potter bought Hill Top Farm and made it famous in *Jemima
Puddle-Duck*. *Tom Kitten* and *The Roly-Poly Pudding*
recorded the garden, *The Pie and the Patty-Pan* is the song
of praise of Sawrey village through which the action roams,
though only in *Benjamin Bunny* is the village mentioned
by name. *Ginger and Pickles*, the last of the Sawrey stories,
describes the crowded, many-odoured little village shop.
They are not to be minimized, the miniature denizens of this
Beatrix Potter world. Did they not at one point actually
bring their creator into politics and against Free Trade
at that? On the other hand one must keep one's head.
This small created world of interesting innocence and fresh
and dewy happiness is insidiously beguiling. But this artist
refused to be taken too seriously. Miss Janet Adam Smith,
in a sensitive article in *The Listener*, placed her with her
painted illustrations, within their childish sphere, in the same
company as Palmer, Calvert, Bewick and a host of earlier
English artists. "Great rubbish, absolute bosh!" was the
subject's reaction. Mr. Graham Greene wrote a fascinating
analysis of her art, drew analogies with Henry James and
Shakespeare, and spoke of vintage years in comedy and

of a dark period. The essay drew from Miss Potter what
Mr. Greene described as a somewhat acid letter. "She denied
that there had been any emotional disturbance at the time
she was writing *Mr. Tod*; she was suffering however from the
after-effects of 'flu. In conclusion she deprecated strongly
'the Freudian school' of criticism."

Yet, if we proceed carefully there are at least two things
in which she can help even the earnest topographer: in
appreciation of the beauty of the countryside and in the
domestic details of farm life in the district. Her biographer,
Margaret Lane, in that delightful book *The Tale of Beatrix
Potter* says: "The lakes, the fells, the stone walls and white-
washed farms that she loved are drawn, on their modest
scale, almost with the emotional feeling of a Constable."
(Danger lurks even under such expert guidance! Constable,
as some two dozen sketches in the Victoria and Albert
Museum show, failed notably, as did Girtin and others, with
the lakeland scene.) Beatrix Potter's commemoration of
interiors is, however, a triumph of poetic realism. As Miss
Lane puts it:

> A well-scrubbed flag floor, a rag rug of many colours, a
> saucepan on the hob and a flat iron heating against the bars
> of the range . . . Beatrix was in love with every circumstance.
> Nothing, not the pattern of an oven door nor the design of a
> crochet kettle-holder, escaped her . . . The domestic group of
> her books are perfect records, in their way, of a simple life
> which still exists on the fells . . . In this world, life centres in
> the kitchen, round the fire, where Tom Kitten's mother sets
> her dough to rise under a clean blanket and Tiggy-Winkle airs
> her linen and heats her irons. There is always a polished steel
> fender and a rag rug; there are tin canisters along the mantel-
> piece, a crown-lidded teapot (relic of Edward the Seventh's
> coronation) on the hob, and a kettle-holder hanging from a
> nail. Crochet wool anti-macassars in faded colours soften the
> backs of the favourite chair and the hard horsehair sofa under
> the window. There are geraniums and Creeping Jenny on the
> sill; and tea, when it is spread on a clean cloth on the kitchen
> table, will include a nicely baked pie in a pink and white dish,
> milk in a patterned jug and a pat of yellow butter on a dinner
> plate. One feels that the dairy, with its stone shelves and white-
> wash, is not far away, and that upstairs the bedrooms will have

flowered wallpapers covering the beams, and will be fresh and tidy, with decent china ewers and basins and cane-bottomed chairs.

The authoress Beatrix Potter, having become famous in America and on the Continent, became without misgiving Mrs. Heelis, of Sawrey, influencing, as a farmer, the country-side around her for thirty years. Many themes might appropriately be discussed more generally because they arise so naturally out of her life—the National Trust, for instance, to which she gave Tilberthwaite Farm, the large Monk Coniston estate, stretching from Colwith Bridge to Carrs and southwards to the village of Coniston, Troutbeck Park, and many other farms and cottages she had restored. In all, the Trust holdings in the Lake District were increased by her by about 4,000 acres. It was at Troutbeck that she was able to foster her great interest in Herdwick sheep. Since, however, her books have given us the entrée to farm-houses, it may be more appropriate, since we shall encounter so many of them, to pause for a moment on the general theme of lakeland farms.

Those bequeathed by Mrs. Heelis, and others owned by the Trust, covering now a considerable acreage include many typical old Lakeland farm-houses. Town End Farm at Troutbeck in Westmorland displays many common charac-teristics. It had been occupied for over 300 years by the descendants of the yeoman who built it and still contains the furniture which in the seventeenth and eighteenth cen-turies its owners made and stamped with their initials. It has the cylindrical chimneys we shall see at Coniston Old Hall, Dalegarth, and elsewhere; rubble walls, mullion windows (in this case of wood), slated roof, stone-flagged floors, huge fireplace recess and plenty of oak in beams, panelling and cupboards. Many, even of the smaller farmsteads and cot-tages, have been occupied by the successive generations of one family, each of whom has made additions, now weathered into a harmonious unity. Wordsworth, announcing that he was about to use a strong expression said (mildly enough I should have thought) that such dwellings may rather be said to have grown than to have been created; to have risen, by an instinct of their own, out of the naked rock—"so little is

there in them of formality, such is their wildness and beauty".
The poet's eye guided his observation though, and he goes on:

Among the numerous recesses and projections in their walls,
and in different stages of their roofs, are seen bold and harmonious effects of contrasted sunshine and shadow. It is a
favourable circumstance that the strong winds, which sweep
down the valleys, induced the inhabitants, at a time when the
materials for building were easily procured, to furnish many of
these dwellings with substantial porches; and such as have not
this defence are seldom unprovided with a projection of two
large slates over their thresholds. Nor will the singular beauty
of the chimneys escape the eye of the attentive traveller.
Sometimes a low chimney, almost upon a level with the roof,
is overlaid with a slate, supported on four slender pillars, to
prevent the wind from driving the smoke down the chimney.
Others are of a quadrangular shape, rising one or two feet
above the roof; which low square is often surmounted by a
tall cylinder, giving to the cottage chimney the most beautiful
shape in which it is ever seen. Nor will it be too fanciful or
refined to remark that there is a pleasing harmony between a
tall chimney of this circular form and the living column of
smoke ascending from it through the still air. These dwellings,
mostly built . . . of rough unhewn stone, are roofed with slates
which were rudely taken from the quarry before the present
art of cutting them was understood, and are therefore rough
and uneven in their surface, so that both the coverings and
sides of the houses have furnished places of rest for the seeds
of lichens, mosses, and flowers. Hence buildings which in their
very form call to mind the presence of nature, do thus, clothed
in part with a vegetable garb, appear to be received into the
bosom of the living principle of things as it acts and exists
among the woods and fields; and, by their colour and shape,
affectingly direct the thoughts to that tranquil course of nature
and simplicity, along which the humble-minded inhabitants
have, through so many generations, been led.

The latest historian on the English farm-house, Mr.
Martin Shaw Briggs, almost omniscient, except that he is
under the strange impression that Wordsworth was a York-
shireman by birth, points out how little even an authoritative architectural writer can add to Wordsworth's discerning
analysis of the relation between Lakeland landscape and

E.L.—5

The Gullery, Ravenglass

domestic architecture. The characteristic slate encountered
everywhere, though greyish in colour and quarried largely in
Lancashire, is what is known as "Westmorland blue".

Our road drops to the wooded shores of tiny Esthwaite
Water at the head of which is Hawkshead. It is the strangest
Chinese puzzle of a little town. In many houses your roof-
level is your neighbour's ground floor, or you rest similarly on
someone beneath and in front. If it was possible to join a
building to another the builders did. The resulting improvised
jumble is like a large-scale version of those models in which
the intelligence of mice is tested by their ability to get out.
Stone passages lead into each other and beyond or suddenly
back to where you started. A courtyard may be pentagonal,
two walls may be at an angle of 75 degrees or 25. Nothing is
square or at right angles. The penthouse or simple cottage
for which you are looking may be over the passage in which
you are standing or underneath. You may have to go outside for the stairs to the bedroom. It is fascinating but seems
to have affinity with nowhere else in the district, to be in fact,
if the words convey what I mean, quite foreign in a very
English way. The churchyard provides the best vantage
point from which to grasp the layout of the place. It is
on an eminence of characteristic abruptness. From there
you see that Hawkshead grew by improvisation. Each
individual step had its own logic. The place as a whole
none. Today, mercifully, it would be impossible to rationalize
it.

Wordsworth was educated at the Grammar School from
1778 to 1783 and the house in which he lodged occupies two
levels of a typically odd-shaped corner. It was on the nearby
water of Esthwaite that he enjoyed those boyhood pleasures
of which surely the sounds still echo for us and colours glow
more vividly than those that any other writer has caught in
words and launched again to move unborn generations—the
wind in the distance, the voices on the ice, the click of a lifted
cottage door-latch and against the silence of the lake, one
summer night, almost the sound of a boy's heart beating
faster as the huge peak of Wetherlam rose between his boat
and the stars.

A slight diversion from the road to Coniston leads one to

Tarn Hows. Just as Hawkshead has a strange individual interest, Tarn Hows always seems to me to focus in the smallest miniature landscape the most intensely character- istic Lake District scenery; and just as the district as a whole, small by alpine standards, impresses because of the propor- tion that everywhere prevails so that quality is repeated where the tarn lies in its mountain setting. It is rightly famous as a beauty spot and now that it is secure for the National Trust, thanks along with many other gifts to Sir S. H. Scott, more and more people make it the object of their outing. They are passionately implored not to leave litter, and though they may rob the individual visitor of his solitude they cannot spoil the view which is unmarred by telephone post or pylon, or, from the little hill on the south side of the road, by sight of road or house. Coniston Water stretches in the distance with Coniston Fells beyond, then Wetherlam, Bowfell, the Langdale Pikes, Helvellyn, Fairfield, Red Screes and the Troutbeck fells. Everywhere the bracken covers them in autumn with reddish gold. Few who feast the eye on its perfection remember that it is to a large extent a man- made beauty spot, for the tarn itself is partly artificial and most of the trees that frame it are conifers, some of them planted and the rest of them seedlings that have sprung up from earlier plantations. So the creatures called men are really quite entitled to come in their motor-cars and gaze on beauty which they have aided nature to create. Familiarity cannot stale it any more than it can music like the 'cello air with which Saint-Saens' swan, heart-easing as ever, is heard in some programme of more ambitious but not necessarily more beautiful music. The swan, or the slow tune's evocation of it, glides harmoniously enough into the recollection of Tarn Hows.

From the heights at the upper end of Coniston the lake reveals itself as akin to Windermere in wooded opulence against a mountain background. It is smaller and more homogeneous. The village lies across the water at the foot of Coniston Old Man and Yewdale Crags about half a mile from the head of the lake. The road along the east side yields fine views across the water to bare but noble fells behind. Brantwood, the house where Ruskin lived for thirty years, is particularly well placed to command this prospect. The house is the chief object of pilgrimage on this side of the lake and dominates one's interest in Coniston. Wordsworth, if one may without discourtesy put it that way, is all over the place. Ruskin is most intensely evoked here. Both were giants in their day. In the date of their deaths they neatly divided the last century into halves. We, whom time has carried half-way through the succeeding century may still stretch to measure ourselves in some ways against the first writer, and try to drive away the rats that scurry over the remains of the other in this his fallen day.

You approach Brantwood, perhaps murmuring to yourself half-remembered incantations from Ruskin's prose about where the swallow leans on the sirocco, or something about the witch of the Alps flinging the spun tresses of the Rhône glacier for ever from her snow; alternatively, in which case you cease to be me, you may be asking in the unencumbered contemporary way: "Who was Ruskin?" He was—oh, he was only . . . well he was (don't they teach you anything nowadays? And the taxes we pay for education!) . . . he was Ruskin! And who was he? Well, when G. M. Young wrote the essay in which he tried to stake the claims for the greatest Victorian he paused long and seriously on Ruskin before finally deciding on Bagehot. (Who's Bagehot? Who's G. M. Young?—Oh, what's the use? Be off to the next youth hostel!) Brantwood is for the initiate, preferably necrolatrous. But he needs to be one who can stomach the smell of sulphur and decay, the odour of the tomb; one with nerves strong enough to face the decline in half a century of a prophet in his day to a figure in a niche in the pantheon of "Eng. Lit." whose books encumber the shilling stall and whose name is known to but could not be annotated by the young of today. To those dim indescribables (God bless them! He inscrutably will!) I will undertake to demonstrate that Wordsworth's is the greatest mind, the one whose generalizations have (all comic failures thrown in) remained the most enduringly true (let Mr. Aldous Huxley drag them to the tropics to try them in an alien climate) of any that have been made by all the geniuses this inexhaustible thirty by thirty miles of country has yet inspired. I would despair at having to re-create (for

the same dear questioners) from Brantwood today what
Ruskin was.

This undistinguished conglomeration of a house into which
he extended a charming eighteenth-century cottage was the
chosen and self-created abode of the apostle of beauty, the
artist-saint. His one and unexpected disciple, Proust, said
that for Ruskin the beauty to which he consecrated his life
was not an object for enjoyment made to charm him but a
reality infinitely more important than life itself and for which
he would have given his own. Yet apart from the pictures
and the view from the windows it is the ugliness of everything that assaults the senses. The large studio he built on
has the worst features of a disused billiard room, a forgotten
railway station and an atheistic church. The utter absence
everywhere of beauty of design in things like household
appointments and furniture! Did the political economy he
preached have as much bearing on the reality of affairs as this
has to beauty? And underneath all his teaching on personal
matters one cannot help feeling grows the great hollow,
the tremendous, mendacious conspiracy with himself and the
world about his sex life. His age and his parents and the cruel
fate dealt him in his disastrous make-up made him bogus.

Less than sixty years ago this house was full of the
crowded life of the honoured patriarch. From the recollections of those who knew him, A. C. Benson, Canon Rawnsley,
W. G. Collingwood and others, we can re-create the living
scene. There was generous hospitality in the rooms whose
windows framed the views of the lake and the hills; wine was
allowed but not tobacco. Beauty was worshipped and it was
not considered improper for the housemaid to draw attention
respectfully to the fact that there was a particularly fine
sunset on. The morning post would be a mountainous cross-
section of the great world outside to whom he meant so
much—private friends, admirers, students, critics, religious
fanatics, cadgers—all to be answered. Then the morning
would get under way, with pictures to examine, drawings,
shells, casts to be arranged. The gardens and immediate
vicinity were charming. After lunch Ruskin would lead a
party on a walk when they might see his agricultural experiments, his private garden or perhaps the ice-house—a

misguided attempt to provide a supply of ice for the district by tunnelling at enormous expense into the rock. At even greater expense the best ice was introduced, but when at last the place was opened only a puddle of dirty water was disclosed. One shrinks from exploiting the symbolism of that failure.

His eightieth birthday focused the veneration—the flowers, the letters, the telegrams that lay in heaps, the address on vellum signed by the Prince of Wales, the Archbishops, the Royal Academicians, the various Ruskin societies and many others, addresses from the University of Oxford, the London Ruskin Society and the Coniston Parish Council . . . honour, love, obedience, troops of friends.

Who are we, gaping, irreverent intruders, as lacking in veneration as the scene-shifters after the curtain has come down, or the ghouls into which we all seem to turn when at last the great house is to be sold up, everything at auction, and the touts and the harpies finger and prowl, and here and there one stands who remembers and feels at any moment he will be sick. What has happened? Is anyone to blame? That question can answer itself or be wasted. One feels immeasurably sorry for everybody—the dissolution has been so inevitable and complete. W. G. Collingwood, writing with a full heart at the time of Ruskin's death in 1900, describes how he liked to be visited by children and to hear them call him "Di Pa" (Dear Papa). Fifty years later Mr. Peter Quennell is not lacking in compassion when he writes:

> He had loved children; and it is sad to learn that in the twilight of his old age some children came to dread him. There he sat on the lawn at Brantwood, an ancient, long-bearded figure, stared at them with eagle eyes and beckoned them incessantly; but if they approached, their reception was very often startling, and the words "Bow-wow—Damn!" pronounced with dreadful emphasis, might send them scurrying homewards.

Even Professor Acland had to give ground when, hearing that his old friend declined to eat, he ventured to take him up a fried sole with which, for thanks, he was struck across the face! Such emerging details are of course among the mildest of the disclosures in our day. The works of Mr. Quennell and

of Admiral Sir Wm. James are not on view among the appreciative literature on sale at Brantwood. The successive
disclosures were painful for anyone to read; they must have
been infinitely so for the hierophants and the disciples. One
feels sorry for them. It must be hard for them to realize that
what time is exposing is the limitation of their outlook in their
day. The process of erosion will never, I imagine, reduce their
Colossus to nullity.

I even feel sorry for the lad I was myself thirty years ago (is
just a touch of the most nauseating vice permissible at that
interval?) when I think how I saved my precious shillings to
buy *Modern Painters* and *The Stones of Venice*, and actually
traced, laboriously, those Gothic arches, and looked for them
and the Venetian traceries in the streets of Bolton where alas
I found them—on for instance the Gas Offices in Hotel Street
and the turrets of the cotton kings' palaces along the Chorley
New road of which Ruskin is as certainly the misunderstood
inspirer as he is of the museum-like houses in Bradmore Road,
Oxford. I did not know when I set out to toil after him that
Ruskin had himself realized that his encouragement of such
mannerisms had been responsible for some of England's
ugliest buildings, and, as he himself put it, "mottled our manufacturing chimneys with black and red brick, dignified our
banks and drapers' shops with Venetian tracery and pinched
our parish churches into dark and slippery arrangements for
the advertisement of cheap coloured glass and pantiles". Yet
I do not regret having read his books. Instead I am immeasurably grateful to him, apart from many other things, that he
taught me early in life to look at and enjoy the sky. And if
extreme old age should be my unlikely sentence I have always
thought it might even be made enviable on some pattern such
as his when he would sit for long hours—the empty chair
still stands in the same window bay at Brantwood—and
watch the changing light on the lake and the hills. At times
his mind would be blank; at others his thoughts would form
and re-form like the fire-flies among the scented thickets of
which he wrote at the end of *Praeterita*:

> How they shone, moving like fine-broken starlight through
> the purple leaves. How they shone through the sunset that
> faded into thunderous night as I entered Siena three days before,

the white edge of the mountainous clouds still lighted from the
west . . . and the fireflies everywhere in sky and cloud rising
and falling, mixed with the lightning, and more intense than
the stars.

Collingwood describes the old man thus in some most moving
pages, and on the evening of his death noted that at the end,
"sunset and evening star shone bright above the heavenly
lake and the clear-cut blue of Coniston fells". Life in the end
spares us nothing we are capable of bearing and Mr. Quennell
is a great one for life. His last glimpse is of the Professor
complaining to two ardent Ruskinian disciples that his
beloved Turners had faded. "*There* was a picture that would
never fade," declared Mrs. Severn, it may be a little too
brightly, pointing through his study window. "For *me* it has
faded," said the author of *Modern Painters*; and his young
disciples felt that the time had come to bid him good-bye.

You escape with relief from Brantwood. The world outside
is waiting, the mist perhaps rising from the snowy ridges of
the Old Man, Dow Crag, Wetherlam, as on the last time I
turned to them thus and they seemed strangely to make a
giant affirmation to the effect that the earth is the Lord's and
the fullness thereof and not Mr. Ruskin's, or anyone else's.
And I thought of the great sanity of Wordsworth's description of himself as "the transitory being that beheld this
vision". If that does not suffice it is still much. And so far it
has not proved assailable as an account of any of us.

If this seems too long an expatiation and you turn im-
patiently to Symonds for the way back to the hills you will
find him stating baldly that Coniston has had four main
sources of its wealth—copper, and the Herdwick sheep, and
John Ruskin, and Dow Crag. We agreed to run at least one of
the hares we put up in each section. Here Ruskin had it.

We approached Coniston via Hawkshead and Tarn Hows,
which can also of course be visited from Coniston, and I have
thereby revealed that our base has really been Windermere.
Coniston, apart from the lake itself, seems in some ways fated
to be a lovely garment divided between Windermere and the
Duddon valley. Even the Coniston or Lancashire fells are
disputed. For them Coniston is the best centre, asserts
Baddeley. Symonds declares it is a delusion to think that to

climb them you must stay in Coniston. They are as near to Dunnerdale which gives an incomparably better approach. "No one will wish to climb on to the Old Man from Coniston twice, trailing in dudgeon round his excoriated flanks; these indecent outlines of Coniston have a touch about them of industrial Lancashire, or of North Wales, and one treads gingerly among the exposure of his vital organs. But walk along the two-mile ridge from Carrs southward ... and all the scattered indecency is out of sight."

Before following this strenuous advice, note that the road up Yewdale, the valley which leads north-east from Coniston, goes over Oxenfell to Skelwith Bridge and so to Ambleside, and is the way out at that end. Yewdale Beck itself, letting the road go its way over Oxenfell, flows from the north-west along a narrow enclosed valley at the head of which Tilberth-waite Fells, Gill, and High and Low farms constitute a strangely remote scene, more characteristic of Scotland than the Lake District. The Gill is a ravine, almost 200 yards long. If you achieve the perilous scramble to the top you can walk to the top of Wetherlam and from there join the track from Carrs to the Old Man. The ascent from Coniston is a popular climb and the view from the summit is justly famous. In addition to a fine array of peaks and the wooded settings of Coniston Lake and parts of Windermere, the view includes great stretches of sea. Fleetwood is visible across More-cambe Bay. Then come the broad sands of the Duddon estuary, Black Combe, industrial Furness, the sea again and the Isle of Man in the distance.

Coniston village is beautifully situated but marred by mining. The copper mines you pass at Gillhead Bridge on the way up to the Old Man were worked by German miners under Queen Elizabeth I. Tennyson occupied Tent Lodge in 1848, and Coniston Old Hall, with its round chimneys, once shelt-ered, I like to think, that Countess of Pembroke "Sidney's sister, Pembroke's mother" who inspired a perfect epitaph.

E.L.—6

The Gateway leading out of the Churchyard, Hawkshead

CHAPTER IV

The Duddon Valley

THE River Duddon issues from its valley—Dunnerdale as it is called—and in what Wordsworth describes as radiant progress towards the Deep, does not as he accurately observes hurl itself precipitously from steep to steep but *now* expands (majestic, much apostrophized Duddon!) over smooth, flat sands and glides in silence with unfettered sweep.

We may take *now* to be Duddon Bridge, with its double arches, a great vantage point from which to view what lies before and after. If you look inland you look up between the jaws of one of the greatest of the Lakeland valleys. Like its westerly neighbour Eskdale, it has an interest and beauty of proportion that would have meant great popularity had the valley contained a lake. The two losses together may be said to constitute a gain. As you look up the valley you have Cumberland on the left, Lancashire on the right. Behind you is the salt marsh of the estuary, of which the Solway is the great prototype. The marsh stretches far out in the estuary where in the Middle Ages the industry of manufacturing salt flourished. The monks in particular stored large quantities of salt and traded what they could preserve from the marauding Scot. St. Bees were among those who had their pans in the Duddon estuary and the tenants of Clifton in Westmorland paid a boon service to go to St. Bees yearly to fetch salt. Today near the industrial coast the marsh may be "bleared, smeared with toil; and wear man's smudge and share man's smell", but the marsh thrusts long fingers surprisingly far up the valley, leaving the soft turf that the tide covers and bringing the characteristic flowers, scurvy-grass and thrift, sea plantain, sea milkwort, saltwort, sea lavender and sea aster. Yet there almost beside them are oak, ash and birch, daffodil woods and the hazel and cherry of the mountain valleys. Duddon Bridge is also a good point to read part of the story of the rocks which here links with that of the sands, for the broken fragments that become pebbles and then merge into the sand and silt of the estuary are of that very volcanic rock which constitutes so great a part of the finest Lake District scenery; the great skylines and craggy ridges, and noble giants of the great central fells, not only the Scafell massif out to Horn Crag but the Gable and Kirk Fell, Pillar Fell, Scoat Fell and the Steeple, Great End, Glaramara, the Langdale Pikes, and Bow Fell and many others. The extraordinary thing is that this volcanic rock gives its knobbly, distinctive appearance to the landscape not only in the central massif but even at a few hundred feet. That first Lancashire eminence on your right, Bank End, is only the last most seaward point, the point of disintegration and surrender to silt and tide of a twelve-mile range of volcanic mountain eminences, dealt down after the creation of Esk Hause and Bow Fell and Crinkle Crags in some cosmic overplus, across Wrynose and Wrynose Bottom (Duddon flowing below), tumbling one after the other, Cross Friar, Dow Crag, Coniston Old Man, Stickle Pike, down to diminutive Bank End. This is the south-eastern wall of the great volcanic oblong. If, from Duddon Bridge, you turn farther to the right towards Coniston you see the lower tops of the Upper Silurian rock which came after the volcanic period and covered the volcanic rocks under a layer probably 15,000 feet deep. "Coniston limestone" is one of the Silurian strata. It resulted in the gentler, quieter country typical of Windermere and Coniston. Only as the more recent rock wore away were the more angular outlines and skylines revealed. Look in exactly the opposite direction from Duddon Bridge and you will see, in Black Combe, the oldest of the rocks, the Skiddaw slate that underlay the volcanic rocks. Because such a hotch-potch of igneous matter dissolves in different ways and at different speeds the road up the valley, compounded as it is of these rocks, turns and climbs and dips and contorts in endless surprises. River and road run moreover like a married couple for ever parting but for ever attracted together, like the Hero of Strauss's *Heldenleben*, and his vivacious, unpredictable spouse, sometimes progressing harmoniously side by side, occasionally breaking away if only for the joy of reunion, and after the storm and stress living on the recollection of achievement.

From where it flows beneath us at Duddon Bridge to Cockley Beck near its source, where we propose to trace and then leave it, the River Duddon in about ten miles traverses several stretches of quite strikingly contrasted country. The first stretch is from here to Ulpha Bridge. The road rises through rich woodlands, up on to the open moor and has a fine run untrammelled by fences.

The rural nature of this valley had been threatened at intervals through the centuries before the nineteenth clutched industrial Cumberland in its decisive embrace. A smelting furnace was started at Duddon Bridge in 1737 and there was a forge at Ulpha in 1625 worth £300 a year to its Hudleston owners. The iron mines in 1688 were consuming £4,000 worth of timber in the forges. Today the place knows them not, nor their whereabouts, and in Ulpha old bobbin mills suggest only a fairy-tale atmosphere which is strengthened by other curiosities of which one hears tell in the valley —a huge push-halfpenny table, a bar that opens and closes in a curious way—and by the picturesque distribution of the cottages, by the old stone bridge that brings us over the river, and by the little church perched on its rock with lych-gate and handcuffs in the vestry recalling the days when the sexton was the policeman. Legend contributes the lady from the ruined tower of Ulpha Old Hall who in fleeing from a wolf was drowned in the ravine known as The Lady's Dub, a dub being the local name for deep clear pools—what Wordsworth called "bright liquid mansions". Up by the end of the Traveller's Rest the road climbs steeply that will lead, when the time comes, over into Eskdale. Meanwhile from Ulpha to Dunnerdale Brig stretches the most kindly section of the valley, road and river harmonious companions, and the farms and cottages more numerous. At the end of this reach stands Wallabarrow Crag, crowned with a small Druid circle and clothed in season with heather—hinting at austerities ahead. Between the point on the map marked Hall Dunnerdale and Seathwaite Bridge, road and river behave with Straussian virtuosity. The river plunges into its gorge which has room for nothing else, so the road, improvising, strikes up the valley of Tarn Beck, crosses and leaves it with a pirouette in which it is arrested in mid-air and handed to safety by a gate, thereafter one of the gates of your life, climbs steeply round Holling House Tongue and confronts you with a "scream point" of great beauty. After preoccupation with valley and road you can suddenly look back down Duddon Gorge and forward and around at the open fells.

We have, however, just passed without sufficient attention the village of Seathwaite. The church of which Wordsworth wrote has since been re-built but is not alien in its simplicity to the character of its famous incumbent, Wonderful Walker. His story is well known, but so far from becoming a mere curiosity of a forgotten day it may be read again so long as anyone retains an interest in what men live by in the most searching sense, and intelligence enough always to investigate sceptically the claims of "progress".

His story is told and documented by Wordsworth in his notes on the Duddon Valley sonnets and can be read there in interesting and extensive detail with the aid of a powerful magnifying glass. Briefly, Walker was born in 1709 and died at the age of ninety-three, as did his wife, in 1802. He was one of twelve children, was considered an ailing one and therefore set to learn the three R's and thus became a schoolmaster at Loweswater. He acquired a knowledge of the classics, was ordained, and at the age of twenty-six became curate of Seathwaite. His stipend was £5 a year, and the appointment carried with it a cottage to which he brought a bride who bore him eight children. By the spinning and weaving which he taught them they helped in time to increase the family income to £20 a year. He grew his own food, sheared his sheep, tanned their hides, made clothes, boots and clogs, and tramped to market with his wool even in the depth of winter. During his sixty-seven years as curate he was thus schoolmaster, lawyer, doctor, brewer, spinner, tailor and a hundred other things. For eight hours a day he would sit in the chapel which also served as school and where the altar was the only desk, spinning as he taught. He lived frugally but extended hospitality to the stranger, educated his children, and left £2,000. There have been others, different in detail, but like him. Indeed Wordsworth described him as:

> A pastor such as Chaucer's verse portrays,
> Such as the heaven-taught skill of Herbert drew,
> And tender Goldsmith crowned with deathless praise.

Did they live by values jettisoned today? Walker at least showed that a man may, on the most exiguous means, live life abundantly who lives it "true to the kindred points of heaven and home".

Wordsworth may also still be allowed the appropriate word on Seathwaite's Stepping Stones, one of the four or five sets on the Duddon:

> Stone matched with stone
> In studied symmetry, with interspace
> For the clear waters to pursue their race
> Without restraint.

It would need a genius more akin to Hieronymus Bosch or Salvador Dali to portray the next crossing to which the most incomparable stretch of the river is leading us—Birks Bridge. Watching the water from the open fell road you gather the noisy river has thrust and spluttered, fallen, splashed, and swum over rocks, past rowans and birches from some notable crisis. Surprisingly the Duddon at Birks Bridge is a microcosm a few yards square. Memory may evoke it as an affair of dark, clear, still pools; you may swim, or hang over the pack bridge that springs over the little chasm and meditate on deep waters; and when you come next time you may find it plaiting thrashing tails of foam, threatening human life— and yet always, in the midst of that strange pool, enduring all, apparently indestructible, is the startling rock effigy of a human leg, unmistakable, inexplicable, whether seen through the clear waters of a summer pool or assailed by winter turmoil. It is variously interesting in my experience. Its lapidary immortality is always curious to behold on the spot; and once I heard it recalled, with a strange gruesomeness, by two barmaids in Barrow who had apparently once ventured thus far into the interior. The leg, normally to them an

attractive symbol but in this case isolated and somehow
terrifying, had exercised on them a sort of Jamesian horror
which had sent them hurrying back to Barrow reconciled to a
bed presumably, apart from the appropriate quota, leg-less.

Such is the virtuosity of the Duddon that the next two
miles from Birks Bridge to Cockley Bridge are almost aus-
terely different from the excitements of the lower reaches.
Through a flat-bottomed, uneventful valley, the river washes
as quietly along as Itchen or Cam through their lusher
meadows, though even these elevated pastures, 700 feet
higher than Duddon Bridge where we began, are bright in
summer with harebells, tiny wild violets, the blue speedwell
Dorothy Wordsworth loved, the celandine for which her
brother opted. Of such mountain pastures as these Norman
Nicholson says: "Even the flowers which are also common in
the lowlands—wood-sorrell, dog violet, sweet violet, bluebell
(which as in Scotland is normally called the wild hyacinth),
moschatel, with dog's mercury, primrose and enchanter's
night-shade at the edge of woods—seen here have a darker,
richer, look. They all have that rather intense appearance of
flowers which feed among thunder clouds, or of the orchises
which look as though they were sweating blood." When
another poet, Professor Day Lewis, turned critic he became
aware, in fancy, of adjurations such as "Keep off the grass!
Do not pick the daffodils! Property of W. Wordsworth."
The poets still free to enjoy sensuous pleasures have always
found the flowers of the Lake District an inexhaustible
source of delight and of new images. On flowers, as on all
aspects of the natural scene, there seem to be three stages.
There is hearing what Wordsworth said, reacting against
him, and finally seeing things for yourself. That in itself, of
course, is some measure of the force of Wordsworth's impact,
and the Duddon valley provides us with the most extended
exercise, if we care to make it, in the collation of place and
poem. Here before your very eyes is the same scene. Here in
your battered old edition is what the poet said. Cockley
Beck is the point at which to abandon our exploration of the
river which splits into various streams but "rises" as Wordsworth's title-page informs us, "upon Wrynose Fell, on the
confines of Westmorland, Cumberland and Lancashire; and,

having served as a boundary to the two last counties for the
space of about twenty-five miles, enters the Irish Sea between
.the Isle of Walney and the Lordship of Millom''. A stone
marks the three-shire boundary point. The river turns sharply
to the right up Wrynose Pass. The Romans who came over
Hardknott on the left would take this road down to Little
Langdale, as you may if your way lies there.

But we have based our exploration of Duddon on Broughton near the sea. We can return and in the lower reaches,
vary the journey on fell roads that give wonderful views.
Or, since we came in the opposite direction, we may perhaps
that evening at the inn trace Wordsworth's progress as he
recorded it.

He too was impressed in the early stages by the flowers.

> There bloomed the strawberry of the wilderness,
> The trembling eye-bright showed her sapphire blue,
> The thyme her purple, like the blush of Even.

We have already noted that after "the struggling Rill"
had grown "into a Brook of loud and stately march" at
Seathwaite there was a geometrical, almost Johnsonian description, of the Stepping Stones. Upon them Wordsworth
plays out a Raeburnesque, crossing-the-stream mezzotint, the
blushing shepherd-lass, in sweet confusion, accepting her
partner's thrilling aid, whilst frolic Loves on a nearby high
rock "clap their wings for victory".

There are more fancies and fairies but nothing disastrous.
In a series of typical scenes he traces the river's changing
source to the sea. I have already quoted some of his descriptive touches. The cumulative impression gradually pre-
dominates over every detail. The thirty-four sonnets were
begun when Wordsworth was thirty-four and finished when
he was fifty. The final one, *After-thought*, has not often been
surpassed.

> I thought of Thee, my partner and my guide,
> As being pass'd away.—Vain sympathies!
> For, backward, Duddon! as I cast my eyes,
> I see what was, and is, and will abide;
> Still glides the Stream, and shall for ever glide;
> The Form remains, the Function never dies;

While we, the brave, the mighty, and the wise,
We Men, who in our morn of youth defied
The elements, must vanish;—be it so!
Enough, if something from our hands have power
To live, and act, and serve the future hour;
And if, as toward the silent tomb we go,
Through love, through hope, and faith's transcendent
   dower,
We feel that we are greater than we know.

The future hour that Wordsworth served is ours in turn.
What of *le vierge, le vivace, et le bel aujourd'hui*? Time has
made it our Duddon for a brief spell, and grateful though we
may be to share an earlier vision we must look at it with our
own innocent eye in our day.

The last opportunity I had to visit the Duddon valley
happened to be a rainy week-end at the beginning of
November—an unlikely time one might think to surprise any
unexpected beauty in the Lake District. It promised to be an
experience that echoed the despondency of walking holidays
marred, of rain streaming outside and the steamy windows
contracting the view to the cruet and the bottle of sauce, the
empty grate and the tasselled plush table-cloth. By contrast
that week-end in the Duddon valley will live in memory for
an unparalleled display of colour and virtuosity of Nature.
The previous evening held out little promise. A late afternoon walk around Broughton, when we had watched lamps
being lit indoors and the light fade from the subfusc colours
of the houses round the old market square and cross, ended
at the top of the village where High Cross commands four
roads and views in all directions. The hills were massed in
slatey, threatening grey, cloud-capped and dark. The fading
light in the western sky gleamed on headlands and channels.
Dying October promised only rain and the next day
November opened with it.

The miracle occurred in the late afternoon. The grey sky
opened. A bronze-gold sunset happened and the world was
charged as in Hopkins's poem with the grandeur of God,
flaming out "like shining from shook foil", and that glittering
image expressed something about the scene strange and
metallic, but deep, unfathomable. As we motored up the

Duddon valley the sunset behind us made the colours (to steal from another of his poems) "fall, gall themselves, and gash gold-vermilion". The mountain-sides were covered with bracken intense as those chrysanthemums that have forgotten their name of golden-flower and deepened into every sombre red and wine-dark mystery. Then the light in some excess of dying, intensified, shone deeper into dark interiors, so that it flashed from the brass of harness hanging at the back of barns, from cocks' scarlet combs and blue-green, black and gleaming feathers, and from piles of earthy purple swedes. Copper pans in lonely cottages glowed so that beside them lamps lit for the coming night were pale, ineffectual yellow. Hayricks seemed to catch fire, like burning bushes. Swollen with the rain every plunging waterfall could have called itself sour-milk gill. Wordsworth's silver Duddon was green and white and at Birks Bridge dragged lashing manes over the drowned rocks. It was a festival of water, loud enough to fill the valley and to ensure the setting sun had music at the close.

After dark, torrential rain obliterated the last gleam of light from the world. The woman from the village who had come in to help with the washing-up was leaving. When I opened the door to let her out the night was waiting. The wind and the rain leaped at her. In the darkness black mountains stood around, vocal with ravenous swollen, streams. The valley dropped, as though bottomless, to her home.

"Mustn't it be awful", she said, keeping me for a moment whilst she thought of the dreadful possibility, "to live in a town? Fancy having buses and things rushing past, and people all around on the pavement hurrying and jostling—even touching you. And yet they're afraid to go out at night. Oh, I wouldn't like to live anywhere else but here." She started off but called back out of the darkness, referring to her house, "And I'm going in the right direction too." Cheerful, contented, she disappeared. I went indoors to towel my head and brush my hair. I thought with detachment of the leg in the roaring water at Birks Bridge.

CHAPTER V

Eskdale

ESKDALE, though conveniently explored from Dunnerdale, is different in some essentials. It is not shared by
Lancashire but comprises the heart of south Cumberland. Scenery and other things are affected by the fact that
the volcanic rocks give place to granite and also by the
marked change of direction. Duddon is the most westerly of
the valleys that, like Windermere and Coniston, run roughly
north and south. Eskdale is the most southerly of those
western dales which Wordsworth apostrophized as "long,
deep channels for the Atlantic's voice". Up at the head of
Duddon, where from near Cockley Beck, Mosedale strikes
across beneath Crinkle Crags and nearly reaches Eskdale,
only a couple of miles separates the two valleys. By the time
Duddon reaches its sands and Esk the land-locked estuary it
forms with Irt and Mite the two rivers are as far apart from
each other as their end is from their beginning. The sun sets
over the Irish sea and the music that was made for it by the
dub-a-dub syllables of Duddon and Dunnerdale yields to the
variations that the map evokes from the dominant note of
Esk, as the river links Hause, Pike, Gate, Falls, Dale, Green,
Holme, Meols, Estuary—from mountains to sea—Eskdale,
the finest, one is suddenly tempted, impulsively, to pronounce, the noblest and most beautiful of all the valleys.
The others can make out their case when we get round to
them.

From the Duddon valley the best approach by road is the
one that climbs steeply from the Traveller's Rest at Ulpha
to the high, open moorland with fine ranging views before it
drops down to Eskdale Green. Before dropping let us avail
ourselves of a pattern that emerges acceptably enough at this
point of this new section of country. The upland we are

crossing, a great block of south Cumberland between the
valleys of the Duddon and the Esk, runs from Black Combe on
the coast to where Harter Fell presents its rocky face across
Hardknott Pass and looks along Upper Eskdale to Scafell
and the central massif. The valley towards which we are
descending will divide conveniently into the gentle lower
reaches of the Esk between the sea on the left and Eskdale
Green, and the increasingly impressive stretches to the right
up to Hardknott Castle and Pass. Within a mile of our road
across Black Moor is the greatest of the moorland tarns,
Devoke Water.

Black Combe, like some heraldic couchant animal, thrusts
into the sea in an outline that dominates the view whether
from inland or from off the coast, from Scotland or from the
Isle of Man. Because it lies sufficiently far forward to be free of
greater heights it commands the most extensive views, and
can in turn be seen not only from sitting-rooms in Morecambe
but from the tower of Liverpool Cathedral in which the birds
find sanctuary, by passengers for whom the plane comes down
at Speke, or from the mountains of North Wales. This famous,
strangely individual landmark is, as we noted when we looked
at it from Duddon Bridge, the final outcrop in the south of
Cumberland of that Skiddaw slate, the oldest of the rocks
in the district, laid down perhaps 500 million years ago.
Isolated except for the foothills that link it to the Eskdale
fells, it is beaten upon by the Atlantic storms. Its spurs are
deeply eroded by cascading ghylls that freeze in the winter
or gullies that dry up in the summer. Yet here in the Bronze
Age came people from the coasts of France or Spain who left
behind them great circles that were stone altars, or burial
grounds, or inexplicable mysteries. Black Combe carries on
its flank Swinside (Sunkenkirk), one of the three largest of
these structures of which Mr. Norman Nicholson expressively
says: "If we cannot understand the purpose of the circles
surely we can feel the meaning in our bones. There is an
ache of worship in the stones, more primitive, but no less
apparent than in a Gothic cathedral. . . ."

Nearer to Devoke Water the theme of primitive man is
repeated on the strange, impressive ridge of Barnscar. This
is the Borran-scar or ridge of ruins on Birkby Fell. Many

theories are advanced to explain the apparently orderly
groups of stones, the possible broken houses of primitive
type. It is not a Danish city, as is sometimes said, but a
British settlement, and cairns containing Bronze Age burial
urns have been found. But the total effect of the moorland
country around Devoke Water has been compared to that of
Iceland—"huge form and sombre colour contrasting with the
level gleam of sea-line continually reappearing". The lake
itself, a mile long and half as wide, has excellent trout fishing.
To the north-east, Black Moor and Birker Moor lead the eye
up to Harter Fell which in formation belongs to the volcanic
rocks of Dunnerdale, but the fells of Birkby, Stainton,
Wabberthwaite and Corney that look down on Eskdale are
of the granite that prevails until it reaches Black Combe.

The road over the top from Ulpha passes within a mile of
Devoke Water and in toppling over reveals the incomparable
array of the mountains that enclose Eskdale. Immediately
ahead is the back as it were of the Wastwater screes. To the
right, Scafell, Bow Fell, Crinkle Crags, form the magnificent
amphitheatre in which Esk rises. I last walked over this road
on a November afternoon when above the splendour of the
valley and the mountains brilliant white clouds drifted like
summer galleons across the blue sky, lifting, dissolving,
gleaming in the precious brief blaze of sunlight, so that what
was white had imperceptibly become tinged with pink, had
flushed deeper, and drawn apart to reveal in the fading blue
new and incredibly distant regions of cold sea-green and
amethyst, inhuman reaches of space. The puddles in the
road were like pieces of broken mirrors; each glittered with
its fragment of the dissolving sky. Then as we reached the
gate where the descent to the valley begins it was possible
to say:

> However fast you were to run
> you never now could catch the sun
> just fled beyond the mountain height;
> and though from hills still charged with light
> clouds rising in a soundless paean
> exalt the blazing empyrean
> we seek in the contracting gloom
> the valley and the lighted room.

Eskdale, which has such an incomparable valley head among the giants, is saved from tameness as it approaches the sea by the shapely, well-placed mass of Muncaster Fell. The Esk itself rakes the southern side, flowing past Muncaster Castle; the River Mite and the miniature railway to Boot take the north side and end at Ravenglass, once a flourishing Roman port, now a decayed but pleasant, picturesque village on the coast. Muncaster Castle, which originated as a pele tower of refuge from raiders at the port, has had a long and eventful history. At the foot of the fell that divides the river is Eskdale Green, the appropriate village for those who like their grandeur as a background rather than a challenge, although the young for whom the mountains and mountaineering are indeed a splendid challenge will be found at the Outward Bound school from which, as part of their training, parties venture to more dangerous regions. But there are many immediately accessible delights, pleasant walks, interesting farm-houses and villages. Nearby Irton, for instance, has an incomparable Norse cross. The pele tower has become Irton Hall.

Dalegarth Farm or Hall, two or three miles up the valley, though not strictly a pele shows signs of earlier fortification. It is rather a tumbledown place with round chimneys built out of small stones like those at Coniston Hall. Through here you go up to Dalegarth Force, or Stanley's Ghyll. To enjoy it you must have a taste, which is not universal, for ravines as such, for rough going, flimsy, perilous-looking bridges, (there are three with notices of increasing urgency and a final solemn warning that if you break your neck no one else will be given the chance). Do not take your dog. Watching mine turn round on the slender gaping slats high above the roaring torrent cured me of this kind of scenery. I felt he was going to become one of Lakeland's famous dogs at any moment. Such things apart, the scene is remarkable not so much for the 60-feet fall or the volume of water, both of which can be surpassed elsewhere, but for the precipitous cliffs, richly and yet exquisitely clothed with ferns, the towering crags, and the luxuriance of the trees. It earns one of Mr. Baddeley's superlatives: "The finest of its kind in Lakeland."

Resolved, however, to give my own impressions I will

describe my experience of the next notable fall a mile farther on, if only because figures in a landscape are half the interest. In a typical Lake District downpour I left the main road for a nearer view of Birker Force. It seemed to hang high in the air against the black face of the rock. The rough track from which I was looking at it was too swampy for a nearer approach, but the scene was completed by the appearance with his dog of a picturesque old Lakeland farmer, hung round with sacks, the rain streaming from his shepherd's hat.

"It's worth putting up with the rain," I said amiably, "to see the waterfall."

"Get out," he said, or rather shouted at the top of his voice.

"I am just looking at your waterfall," I repeated at the top of my voice.

"Yon's no waterfall. Storm's just brought it down. This is a private road. Mine. Get out!"

"I am not doing any harm," I shouted at the top of my voice.

For a moment he turned aside, leaned over the wall and roared at the cows in some language more primitive even than that with which the last Celts counted their sheep (een, teen, tethera, pethera, etc.). Then he turned round to me with increased rage and shouted—

"I bin to Lunnun to prove this is my land. Get out!"

"Shut up," I said, very firmly and very quietly, relying on his deafness. He twitched his streaming sacks around his shoulders. His face was white with rage and his lips trembled. I might have asked him how he looked forward to the prospect of the Lake District being a National Park. I might, remembering all those worthy old men who inspired Wordsworth, have asked him if he had been gathering many leeches lately. Instead, we stood staring at each other fiercely and finally left, shoulder to shoulder, in that state for which the word dudgeon (high) seems to be reserved. In the gallery of Lakeland figures he has his place.

In many ways Boot is the ideal centre. The valley here is wide. Its structure and symmetry are seen to great advantage. It has everything except a lake, and like the valley of the Duddon probably owes to that fact the preservation of its quiet and age-old characteristics. Even the little narrow-gauge railway that runs in the summer from Ravenglass is no more than an amusing toy. It seems to enjoy a soft spot even in the heart of impersonal British Railways. The architectural indiscretions have in most cases merged into the landscape. The valley so far as we have traced it is rich, almost urbane, though rescued from tameness by the shapely bulk of Muncaster Fell. Beyond Boot the scenery increases in grandeur at every stretch of the river and ends literally nothing short of the highest.

Boot is little more than a road which leaves the valley road at right angles, and near the picturesque bridge over Whillan Beck becomes briefly a village street, with a handful of houses and a simple inn that, either by day or in the light of the one lamp which is such a welcome amenity at night, looks like a Utrillo painting with its miniature white courtyard open to the street, a stubby outside staircase, two benches and in the middle of the cobbles a single graceful Japanese cherry, a welcome denizen that flowers even before the native English may, for which reason it was introduced into the suburbs to persuade Londoners and other town dwellers that there is a season between winter and summer and for the same reason welcome here, "for the Spring comes slowly up this way". But even in winter, in the garden near the bridge the escalonia blooms profusely, with blossoms as pink as the granite and as soft as the rock is hard with strange angularities. Boot stands on Whillan Beck rather than on the Esk and the track over the bridge is immediately enticing. You climb, keeping the stream on your right to Burnmoor Tarn and drop down to Wasdale, for which it provides rather surprisingly the nearest railway, though from Wasdale Head to Boot is about two hours walk. We will reach there later by another route and we will also release any who may care to make the ascent of Scafell from this side, which avoids the crags. This track was one of the old corpse roads. Until the rock-climbers began to make the need more pressing, the nearest consecrated ground for Wasdale Head was Eskdale churchyard, and thither on pack-horses you were borne on the longest journey. On this road you might have met in 1761 a traveller not always remembered when the pioneers

Grasmere Lake, looking north ▸

are recalled, though he travelled with a clearer purpose and left more enduring results—John Wesley, mounted on that most long-suffering nag. If this is the road to which he refers in his *Journal*—and no other fits the description—then as Mr. Bouch points out he was the first person to travel through the central Lakeland passes and leave an account of his journey behind. The old church of the dale, St. Catherine's, lies half a mile from the village, on the bank of the Esk. It has a fourteenth-century east window and font bowl and a fine view of the hills. In the churchyard you may see a heron rise (a jammie-crane the farmer may call it) and watch the sheep leap over the churchyard gate after cropping the turf on the graves of farmers and squires, Tysons and Porters and others, and round the memorial of Thomas Dobson, Master of the Eskdale Foxhounds for more than half a century. From the carved granite a fox and hound peep out and must often watch the living of their kind meet or pass. The dale, particularly from now on, is still the country of farmers and huntsmen. It is more than a hundred years since Squire Sandys's hounds ran a fox from Low Furness to the southern side of Harter Fell, but the fox-hunting men still commemorate the exploit in a song. Change there must be, but it has come slowly. Towards the end of the seventeenth century the churchyard wall had so far fallen into decay that the sheep need not even jump to get in. Although John Wesley passed this way the incumbent in the middle of the nineteenth century was forbidden to exercise his function for many years, being charged with habitual drunkenness, and the huge fourteenth-century font bowl, with its carving and traceries, has come back to the church after straying for sixty utilitarian years in a farm-house.

In times much nearer our own than the Roman occupation the road over Hardknott Pass was called the Wain Gate and as Mr. Bruce Thompson suggests, its heyday was probably during the wool trade boom when strings of pack-horses made their way over here to the great wool-marketing centre of Kendal. Here, perhaps, the traffic would be reasonably sparse, but in many parts in winter and bad weather, carriages and carts did not attempt the road, and riders started early in the morning to get in front of such pack-horse trains, so difficult were they to pass, much as determined motorists today, bound for Scotland or the Lake District, start in the smallest hours to avoid the continuous stream that the internal combustion and the diesel engine create on the great highways. Even today many roads in the north of England involve the motorist in the maximum of difficulty because they were never constructed for him but for pack-horses which could bring to them the requisite amount of our disappearing commodity, leisure. Long may the road over Hardknott, surfaced though it may have been by the invention of that Scottish gentleman from the west of England, John Loudon Macadam, continue to exact its toll from the intrusive motorist by so taxing and overheating his engine, and possibly jangling his nerves, that he may yet learn to walk again. The pushful cyclist is permissible, but what this road can offer should make a gentleman who can ride in the back of a car and smoke a cigar feel a cad.

We haven't yet got there; and I wanted still a word about the past. Those of John Wesley's day saw one thing which we may envy them. After centuries of preparation there emerged, to endure but for a generation or two, the perfect harmony between the natural scene and what man made of it. Whilst, on the other side of Birker Moor and Ulpha Fell, Wonderful Walker's life was spanning the eighteenth century, some aspects of his varied life would be paralleled in many small cottages, now disappeared, where large families were brought up, spinners whilst they were yet children, tending and driving the sheep and somehow growing strong enough to build the stone walls at which we gape incredulously. Spinning and weaving had brought a prosperity to these cottages long before the Woolpack Inn which we are approaching chose a name that symbolized it. The early travellers who beheld only "frightful" and "horrid" and "barren" scenes were describing more than their own vision. Primitive, uncontrolled nature was constantly threatening to re-absorb the pathetic and puny works of man until in the eighteenth century, in such well-drained valleys as Eskdale, prosperity following slowly on the increasing manufacture of cloth at Kendal enabled the builders and the furniture-makers to co-operate with nature before the machine came to dominate it.

The two uppermost farms on the west side beyond the
Woolpack now belong to the National Trust. They are Taw
House, pronounced locally "Tay'us" and deriving from
teathes—tussocks of grass where manure has been dropped;
and Wha House, pronounced "War'us", from wath, a ford.
Opposite the Woolpack, on the other side of the Esk, in a
self-contained, picturesque corner reached by an old pack-
horse bridge, is another delightful property, once an inn,
now the strangely named Penny Hill Farm, also owned by
the Trust. Nearby, the map preserves the name of Spot
How, of which only the foundation stones remain. Mr. Bruce
Thompson, who is vigilant and knowledgeable on these things,
gives its history.

It was pulled down about 1870 and during the process a most
beautiful fourteenth-century ivory diptych came to light, the
carving still in perfect condition. The panels measure $4\frac{1}{2}$ inches
high by $2\frac{1}{4}$ inches broad and there are four separate scenes illustrated: the Crucifixion, preparing Our Lord's body for the tomb,
the Adoration, and the Virgin and Child. This diptych is carefully
preserved by the Benson family, from whom Mrs. Heelis bought
the farm. It is illustrated in the *Transactions* of the Cumberland
and Westmorland Antiquarian Society for 1928 in an article
by Miss Fair, which also describes another diptych at Ulpha,
in the neighbouring Duddon valley. It is of interest to find
these lovely examples of mediaeval carving in what one would
suppose was a remote and uncivilized part of Cumberland.

The farm called Brotherelkeld, or Butterilket, lies right
under the height on which the Romans built Hardknott
Castle, guarding their end of the pass where it climbs off
from Eskdale to drop to Cockley Beck and so on to the
Roman camp at Ambleside. Beyond the farm all is wildness
and solitude, but as you climb to the crag, 800 feet high,
where the site of the camp is still being excavated, the
vanished soldiers seem to people the scene again. On the
green area which perforce had to be levelled on this rocky
protuberance they took exercise and were paraded. Around
are the identifiable remains of the fort and some of the
subsidiary buildings which would be supplemented by others
in wood. The castle stood half-way between Ravenglass and
Ambleside, and apart from the High Street over by Ill Bell

and Troutbeck this is the main Roman interest in the district.
The fort was about 360 feet square, with stone walls, and
corner towers with glass windows. There was a water supply
from the hill behind. Three of the buildings in particular
evoke our common humanity with these men. Here on this
wild outpost was a Roman bath, with the hottest room next
to the furnace and the cold plunge at the other end. Adjoining are what have been conjectured to be a small temple
and a wayside tavern. The guardians having "bent the knee
to Jove and Mars" could raise a glass to the same; and if too
many were raised the steam-room was no doubt then, as
now, the quickest way to get it out of the system.

The fort, like the Romans, was a short-lived interlude. It
was apparently built in one period of reorganization and
abandoned in another in the reign of Trajan who died in the
summer of A.D. 117 on his way back to Rome from the east.
He was succeeded by his kinsman and friend Hadrian, scholar,
artist and soldier, who concerned himself, to the point of
personal supervision and exhausting journeys, with frontier
problems. To solve one of them he altered the wall against
the enemy from the north and carried westwards to that
Bowness where on its south shore the firth of Solway ceases
to be fordable. Apparently he did not re-build Hardknott.
Some small resthouse must have continued to exist by the
road-side but the fort was abandoned. When at the appointed
touch of time the bathroom fell in, it buried a small dog and
its puppies whose brittle bones were found by the excavators
of our own day. The dishes that had broken were left lying
on the floor. They had been made in the kilns in Eskdale—a
local industry run by local people, for the garrison in these
latter years would be recruited from those British, some of
whose blood probably runs in the veins of so many of us, an
occupied and barbarian people then, but destined to survive.

You may stand as they stood and look down the length
of mid-Eskdale, green and wooded. Beyond Ravenglass, the
port the Romans built, is the sea and in the distance the
Isle of Man. The Scafell group rises majestically to the
right, Illgill Head and the ridge of Whin Rigg can be seen
above Wastwater Screes. The other giants are grouped
harmoniously around, majestic, free, sublime. "Wouldst

thou be as they are? live as they do," said the stern voice of
the last century. But as the light creeps up and leaves the
mountain-tops, the far-off twinkle across the darkening sea
of the lighthouse at the northern end of the Isle of Man suddenly seems more kin than the stars or the mountains. The
broken pottery and the little dog, the tavern and the temple,
frail survivals among the volcanic rock on which we stand
and the granite of the foothills, seem more of our order.
Like the autumn gorse that in its season cheerfully, but only
for its season, briefer than that of kissing, flowers on Hardknott Fell, they belong to the little things that as well as
the great triumphs and the great tragedies point man's way;
what Gilbert Murray calls "the beloved and tender and funny
and familiar things that beckon across gulfs of death and
charge with a magic poignancy, the old things that our dead
forefathers loved, *viva adhuc et desiderio pulcriora*—living
still and more beautiful because of our longing". Matthew
Arnold's affirmation and stern counsel about how to be like
the immortals seems to approximate to what we think of as
characteristically Roman. But the Emperor Hadrian who
did well enough in his day also wrote five lines of poetry on
his death-bed—the familiar address to his soul. They have
survived his wall, though they attempt no more than a light
and rather jingling interrogation. *Animula vagula blandula*,
etc. "Little soul, wandering, pleasant, guest and companion
of the body, into what places wilt thou now go, pale, stiff,
naked, nor wilt thou play any longer as thou art wont."

The mountains may elevate, but with the approach of
nightfall and hunger, we seek, as I have already said, the
valley and the lighted room. With the first click of the latch
as you enter, the mood changes, the light dazzles, the smells
are savoury, there are the self-absorbed others. What you
put into words of what you have experienced sounds brittle,
but this is us. When we experience the difficulty of com-
municating with our kind in our time we may perhaps
question the rich evocations of our communings with the
dead. We imagine we can catch the accent of yesterday and
the day before. Can we hear ourselves? Figures in the landscape include the people in the bar.

That evening I was last in Eskdale we ought, at the inn,

to have discussed the Romans. I certainly tried. I was so pleased to meet in the modest hostelry a married couple who had passed us driving down the breakneck spiral of Hardknott Pass. It had filled them with enough trepidation for them to be glad to relax in the valley.

"Hardknott is a wonderful Roman site, isn't it?" I offered.

"Is it? We live on The Wall so we're rather blasé about that sort of thing."

"How interesting. What part?"

"We're Northumberland."

There was something final about that. I don't know why, but one can say "We're Northumberland", just as one can say "We're Yorkshire", or even "We're Cheshire" in a tone and with a hint of implication that I defy anyone to get into "We're south-east Lancashire". Were such nuances discernible, I wonder, among the funny and familiar things when Ravenglass met Ambleside in the wayside tavern at Hardknott.

"Galava did you say you came from? My dear, we're Clanoventa."

CHAPTER VI

Wasdale

ALL the lakes have some affinities. Windermere and Coniston, for instance, have many with each other. Each also has its individuality. Ullswater and Derwentwater are like two elder sisters, each beautiful in a different way. Buttermere and Crummock are the twins of the large family, Loweswater the little one, Ennerdale Water the rather unapproachable one. But Wastwater is the strange one, the least like the rest of the family, the one who mysteriously has something the others have not. Does one ever grow accustomed to Wastwater?

A certain unreality marks the discussion of landscape in almost technical terms and absolute standards of beauty. Perhaps we cannot forget that the taste for mountains is barely two hundred years old. But one element in the beauty of Wasdale is unmistakable. The view as one looks to the head of the valley is the most perfect composition of mountains and water in the district; neither in this country nor in any other have I seen anything more beautiful. Being known it remains inexhaustibly new. Neither the approach over Sty Head nor that from Boot over by Burnmoor Tarn gives the full impression. I would choose always to arrive from Strands and the lower end of the lake, and during those few quiet miles, as in the moments before the arrival of the beloved, savour the being without to enhance the approaching pleasure of being with. The Irt, the pretty river that flows from Wastwater, is crossed twice. The road runs between trees. At times there are splendid glimpses of the mountains, but the lake is hidden. Then the dense woods surrounding Wasdale Hall shut out the whole view, but you pass through a gate, there is a change to a key that aches for resolution, the sky is opening up as the trees fall away, the road runs on to the open fell, and suddenly, like Tristan's irruption in Act Two, it is the moment. You can calm down and take it all in once more.

Even though we have just come through luxuriant woods it is a wild scene. There are no trees ahead; no islands in the lake. The shores have few indentations. The water is the deepest of the lakes. The beauty of the whole scene is bold, major, with no touch of dreariness. I have seen it wonderfully impressive under heavy lowering skies, and radiantly coloured under sun and chasing cloud. Across the lake from our viewpoint are the famous Screes along most of the east bank, rising steeply from the water to a skyline 1,500 feet high. They are undoubtedly the feature that contributes the strangeness to the view. From each gully head, loose stones slide down and pile up backwards from the water's edge, sometimes reaching as far as half-way up. Cathedral architecture has been called frozen music. This strange inverted fan-vaulting is caused by a waterfall of stones, as it were, which is then held immobile, falling and not falling. It seems incredible that one can walk across them, but there is a path which enables one to see the Screes from below. I record with some astonishment that I have done this, but it is a rough scramble, not sufficiently rewarding. The true glory that the Screes offer the walker is the track from south to north along the ridge. There are splendid views of the mountains across the lake and of those ahead, especially the Scafell group, that is if you have eyes to see them, for the compelling attraction of this walk is, strangely, the view beneath your feet. You can keep to the edge. The dark volcanic cliffs have crumbled into fantastic shapes between which the gullies plunge downwards. Black rock seems to be carried into black water far beneath one's feet, whilst the hollow shapes frame beautiful views of the lake.

To return to our viewpoint on the shore. From here the subtle colouring of the fragments that make up the Screes can be appreciated. At the head of the lake the mountains compose the perfect view in such rare symmetry and unity. Each mountain that contributes to the whole is still individual. In the centre Great Gable is precipitous and imposing, a gable indeed; the right forefront is Lingmell, the left

Wasdale Head, looking north-north-west

Yewbarrow, permitting a glimpse of Kirk Fell behind. Above
the skyline on the right is just the beginning of the Scafell
group, but held back as it were by the Screes as though to
release that giant mass would throw all out of harmony, as
indeed it would. Their turn comes presently and to see them
we must advance along the coast road "that the full view
may enter in". At first the country to the left is open, the
steep crags of Buckbarrow rising across a mile of green
meadow. Presently Middle Fell advances, but less formid-
ably, almost to the road and then gives way as guardian
admitting to Bowderdale, a beautiful valley at the head of
which are grouped the giants that stand north-west of Wastwater, Seatallan, the Haycock, the Steeple, Red Pike and
Yewbarrow. They cradle Scoat Tarn from which Nether
Beck runs down to the road, as half a mile farther on does
Over Beck from Low Tarn. The road crosses them as they
enter the lake and runs under Yewbarrow, the steep impressive
frontage to this array of giants. Down Bowderdale and past
Yewbarrow came one of the glaciers which, joining the ice from
Gable and Sty Head, scooped out the deep bed of the lake.

Meanwhile the Screes have yielded place as predominant
feature across the lake to the tremendous cliffs of Scafell and
the crags of the Pike hanging in the foreground of the sky.
Lingmell draws partly across them as you leave the lake and
enter the remote, green valley of Wasdale Head and the
lower end of Mosedale. You may nod to the mountains as
they stand around. You will not be so intimate from any
other green valley with such an impressive array. They
actually come right on to the little green stage with its
mosaic of stone walls, scattered farms, tiny church, footbridge, hotel—Lingmell, Great Gable, Kirk Fell, Yewbarrow.
They are the four most dominating. You could begin the
ascent at once. When we passed Yewbarrow on the road it
stood portal to Bowderdale, partnered by Middle Fell. This
side of it looks across to Kirk Fell where Mosedale, having
come down from the north-west, opens between them on to
the little green plain. Around the head of Mosedale stand
a formidable assembly of mountains. First those like Yewbarrow, Red Pike and the Steeple whose other side looks
down on Bowderdale, then across Windy Gap, the Pillar,

Looking Stead, and then Kirk Fell which looks towards Great Gable. Mosedale Beck rises up there among those mountain heights and from the Wasdale Head Hotel a pony track follows the beck upwards for a while and then turns to climb Black Sail pass and is thus wonderfully away. But before we leave Wasdale Head there is more to take in of what Henry James might say is wonderfully here.

A few hundred yards beyond the hotel, where the pony track crosses a tributary and the beck itself rushes forward through the narrow entrance into Mosedale, is a little force or waterfall which "was named Ritson Force by the late Mr. Baddeley". This style of reference in the posthumous editions of Baddeley's guide savours partly of Queen Victoria's way of referring to herself, partly of a dog bewildered by its own image in a looking-glass. However, cartographer Bartholomew has accepted the episcopal status of the great man (what revenge would he have wreaked on Symonds?) and the name of the force leads us pleasantly to the recollection of a figure in the landscape not to go unrecorded, however familiar. Rowlandson should have painted him.

William Ritson, who was for many years landlord of the Wastwater Hotel, died in 1890 at the age of eighty-three, so that his life spanned most of the last century. Men now living can remember him and he in his turn could remember and tell them stories of the wrestling match with Professor Wilson, of the miserly Eskdale parson and the famous pony-race down Sty Head. He knew Wordsworth and all the famous company whom one is sometimes tempted to refer to as the old gang. Ritson left behind him a string of jokes which crackle more effectively when re-told on the spot in the original dialect. He is probably the best known example of the old type of Cumbrian statesman, and through him one catches glimpses of what life in this remote valley must have been like in earlier generations. How strenuously change was resisted, yet inexorably it had to come. The school marked on the map has been rationalized away, nor can one regret it when one reads that whilst the schoolmaster who was entertained on "whittlegate" terms, that is he boarded at the farm-houses in turn, was held to be good with the children in the spelling, "he thinks if they can spell they can

do all the rest". Towards the end of the eighteenth century
the old type of country vicar, frequently ignorant, always
impoverished, however friendly, had to give way to more
vigorous young men who measured themselves against the
forces of reaction. Man is a thinking reed, however frail,
but whatever the quality of the thought and without
guidance from vicar or schoolmaster some strange and savage
lore must have grown up in this remote little community
which seldom numbered as many as fifty all told, living
entirely under the influence of such impressive natural forces.
Harriet Martineau mentions how strong even in her day was
the curious belief that if a child's arms were washed or its
hair and nails cut before it was six months old it would be a
thief. Superstition, the devil's advocate, must have found
this a happy hunting ground.

When Will Ritson was first told that the precipitous face
of Scafell had been directly climbed he was incredulous.
"Nobbut a fleeing thing", he said, "could get oop theer." In
the course of his life one of the changes he came to accept
was for such feats to become commonplace. At first he used
to think little of rock-climbing as a sport: "What's makkin'
ye fellas fash yersels seea mich aboot climming t'crags?
Isn't t'fells big enough for ye?" And the visitor who happens
not to share the enthusiasm may well mutter some variant
of that sentiment under his breath if he stays at the hotel
to which the sport brought fame and fortune. Any night at
the inn, any night and every night, the talk will be of rock-
climbing. We have encountered a major theme. Buttermere,
Borrowdale, and Eskdale all have their attractions, but
Wasdale is the most central station, the Mecca of the devout.
Four of the finest climbing grounds in Britain are easily
reached, the Pillar, Gable, Mickledon and the Screes. It has
the disadvantage of being so popular that at certain seasons,
particularly at Easter, it is crowded with enthusiasts for the
sport that is, I should have thought, essentially the pastime
of the non-gregarious type. There is something ironic about
seeing a party waiting their turn to advance from the foot
of some fashionable gully or pinnacle rather like a band of
hopefuls waiting for seats when the standing-room-only
notice has been hung out at the cinema. This is not only so

today. I read of similar scenes in climbing books of fifty and sixty years ago.

Nothing is more unpleasant for the beginner than to know that his unskilled efforts are being watched by a censorious crowd who are not only delayed by his slowness but run considerable risk of being injured by the stones which his clumsiness is pretty certain to dislodge. A party of novices will accordingly be well advised if they serve an apprenticeship elsewhere.

The deceptive modesty of this warning should not hide its importance. The words are from the chapter on mountaineering in Collingwood's *Lake Counties*, contributed by W. P. Haskett-Smith, who thus offers appropriate advice on a contemporary situation which nobody did more to bring about than himself, "the father of British mountaineering" as he is sometimes called. It is a case of that father had a father but not much more than a grandfather, for mountaineering and rock-climbing are youthful sports in this country. The forerunners were the fell-walkers and hill-wanderers like Frederick Bowring, who was born in 1823 and lived till 1918. The most eccentric of them was the Rev. James Jackson, "Steeple" Jackson. He was a tall, bearded character who soldiered against Napoleon, joined the Church and astounded his congregation as much by his egotistical verses as by his prodigious feats of walking. In his sixty-ninth year he walked forty-six miles in fourteen and a half hours, followed this up two days later with fifty-six miles in eighteen hours, and after another two days, with sixty miles in less than twenty hours.

The incident which gave him his name illustrates his character in more ways than one. He climbed to the church weathercock to do repairs when the village masons hesitated. When he returned to the ground he recorded the event thus:

> Who has not heard of Steeple Jack,
> That lion-hearted Saxon,
> Though I am not he, he was my sire,
> For I am Steeple Jackson.

As I happen to live in the parish adjoining Rivington, of which he was vicar from 1823 to 1856, I have to record that the steeple is hardly recognizable as such. It looks more like a dove-cote. Fortunately the heights of his real mountaineering conquests are well authenticated. In 1875 he clambered to the top of the Pillar (he was not the first) and dubbed himself "Patriarch of the Pillarites". When he was eighty-two he met his death making his second attempt. On a piece of paper in his pocket, in a bottle he had intended to leave on the summit, were his last lines:

> Two elephantine properties were mine
> For I can bend to pick up pin or plack:
> And when this year the Pillar Rock I climb
> Four score and two's the howdah on my back.

After the day of such pioneer fell-walkers the Alpinists began to look homeward, and men like Leslie Stephen could be met "gangling and prehensile", as Mr. Ronald Clark puts it in his delightful book *The Victorian Mountaineers*, on which I have drawn for much of this history. John Wilson Robinson, an estate agent of Keswick, and Haskett-Smith led in the great era of British mountaineering. Robinson once walked over the principal summits of the Lakes, a total of seventy miles in twenty-four hours. He ascended the Pillar 101 times between 1882 and 1906, taking between thirty and forty ladies to the top during this period, made more than fifty ascents of Scafell Pinnacle and nearly forty of Great Gable. Haskett-Smith, his most constant companion, made his first visit to British mountains in 1882 when he spent nine weeks at Wasdale Head and soon began to pioneer the first ascents of many rocks and pinnacles that today are famous and familiar climbs. It is, however, with the now much-photographed Napes Needle that he is always associated. His account of his solitary conquest of it in 1886 is a classic of mountaineering literature. A photograph of the Needle displayed in Spooner's shop in the Strand fired O. G. Jones, a typical climber of the new generation. "That evening", he recorded, "a copy of the Needle hung in my room: in a fortnight Easter had come round and I found myself on top of the pinnacle." I quote now Mr. Clark's account of a scene historic in the annals of British climbing.

Such was a typical result of Haskett-Smith's discovery. The photograph of the Needle—which was itself later taken as the emblem of the Fell and Rock Climbing Club—became a symbol of the new adventures to be found not beyond the Channel but in Britain itself. Today there are seven regular routes up the Needle, but the magic of its outline still holds. Perhaps the most moving day in its history came in 1936 when Haskett-Smith, then seventy-four, made his anniversary ascent, being led up the summit by Lord Chorley, then President of the Fell and Rock, before an admiring audience of many hundreds ranged around the Dress Circle, the rocky bay on the Napes from which the Needle stands out in all its apparent inaccessibility.

As Haskett-Smith sat down on the uppermost block, a voice from the crowd below urged him to "tell us a story". "There is no other story. This is the top storey", he immediately shouted back, a typical response from a man who devoted much of his life to the curiosities of words, to outlandish facts, and to useless but interesting branches of knowledge.

These ancestral heroes of the sport are only of the day before yesterday. Their photographed faces look down on us from the walls of the hotel, fixed in their period by the fashion in bowler hats and moustaches. The same period flavour marks the now classic writings on the subject. Writers like Lehmann J. Oppenheimer innocently or unselfconsciously describe the climbers in terms which make one rather expect to find them in *The Dolly Dialogues* rather than the Wasdale Head Hotel. Breakfast brings together such characters as the Bohemian, from Cambridge, in knickerbockers, who combs his hair with his fingers, "they say he writes verses and plays . . . an awful clever sort of chap but ye can never mak' out what he's drivin' at". Next to him are three very proper young men in well-starched collars and cuffs. One has a drooping lower lip, another an eye-glass. Most wear jerseys or coarse flannel shirts without collars. The attire of the Christ Church undergraduate is indeed worth recording—a white flannel shirt fastened by a silk cord instead of a stud, and no waistcoat to hide the hardly visible white embroidery down the front.

The patches on his jacket have been so carefully sewn as to be inconspicuous. His watch is carried for safety in a small leathern pouch fastened to his belt, but he is careless enough to wear and endanger the beauty of an exquisite Greek cameo set in a ring of Venetian workmanship, for the scars on the back of his hands show that he has had plenty of close acquaintance with the rocks.

This perhaps I may here repeat is "The Heart of Lakeland" fifty years ago. Meanwhile outside the photographer has been doing the famous barn-door traverse.

Presently with dialogue to suit the costumes they distribute themselves over the peaks where they tend to come on each other's faces appearing over crags on Pillar or Gable. "We've been in Moss Gill taking the direct finish. Which way have you come? Steep Gill? Grand fun along the *arête* isn't it? You know there's a new way now to the ledge below Slingsby's chimney? O.G. found it out. Right up the angle of the cliff." Several more arrive and two of them start a wrestling match in honour of the memory of Professor Wilson. The photographer tells stories of famous climbers and his friend bursts into song. Terrifying antics follow in one of which the strong man insists on unroping, whizzes down the snow and "rolls over into the scree below amidst the laughter of less energetic onlookers". And so back to the hotel and more wise-cracks till after-dinner coffee, smoke, and "criticism slumbers: jokes from Leslie Stephen and Mummery pass as original and raise a laugh for the hundredth time". In the billiards room the athlete demonstrates the passage of the billiards table leg and then the billiards room traverse in which he places his hands on the edge of the table, walks backwards up the wall to within a yard of the ceiling and moves along table and wall simultaneously with hands and feet "avoiding the framed chromolithographs as well as he may". That is only the beginning of the extended performance, but we have time only to note that outside in the cold clear starlight the literary tourist and the Oxford man are "looking up in reverend silence at the dark silhouette of Great Gable, or discussing how best to enter into the spirit of the mountains". Such, according to Lehmann J. Oppenheimer, is a specimen Eastertide day at Wasdale Head.

Perhaps there is some justification for each generation to have a new book describing the Lake District and revealing themselves.

Although we have been absorbed in the mystique of climbing for which Wasdale Head offers such fine opportunities, the mountains that are undeniably best climbed from here are those of Bowderdale, Mosedale and the Screes. The Scafell group and Great Gable are more generally, though less effectively, climbed from Borrowdale, and The Pillar, The Steeple, and The Haycock who sound, if you can hear their names as though for the first time, like three characters from Damon Runyon, belong properly, I maintain, to Ennerdale. And since "for the first time" is how I have been only the latest to try to see the Lake District I will bring in here that delightful master of landscape Mr. Chiang Yee, the Silent Traveller; and I confess that I realize with astonishment that he was amongst us twenty years ago. When he wrote about the English Lakes one caught the knack of seeing the scene through the eyes of a home-sick Easterner. In some places, in Windermere and Derwentwater, there were strange resemblances, but in Wastwater more than anywhere, I think, the prevailing impression was what he called "some half-likeable, half-melancholy strangeness . . ." It is the authentic note even when you know the lake. But if you can catch the eternal freshness of old things, break open the prickly burr of the nut that usage has grown, and release the sharp, sour-sweet savour of the interior, then as you contemplate or evoke in recollection this strange and beautiful lake try out its name as though you had never heard it. Wastwater. Wastwater. Just as the shells that in childhood we used to hold to our ear seemed full of the sound of the sea, the word Wastwater . . . Wastwater . . . seems swept with wind, lonely as nights on bare mountains, eerie with cold depths of the lake . . . Wastwater.

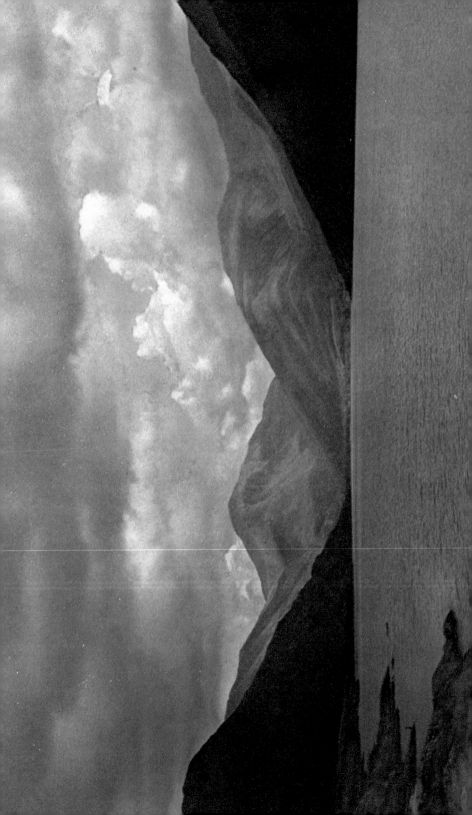

CHAPTER VII

Ennerdale

"IF one dare say it, he did not know his Ennerdale quite
properly." When one realizes that the reference is to
Baddeley then it is clear that even with the deprecating
proviso the words must be those of Symonds. Strangely
enough, not only are the words true but they remain a fair in-
dictment against the guide book now re-incarnated in so many
posthumous editions. Except that these are not dated, this
shortcoming is almost the only one with which the book could
be charged. Perhaps where the master left so noticeable a gap
the anonymous followers hesitate to credit him with their own
words, but there is room for more to be said for this least
known lake and valley. Too many of us do not know our Ennerdale properly. Symonds, on the other hand, knows it so well
that he is able at this point to turn and rend even the great
Bartholomew himself, maker of the map, among many others,
that is our indispensable companion. It is over the rights and
wrongs of Steeple and Scoat Fell and their respective heights.

For he, in his Edinbro' fastness, miscopying perhaps his
survey, places Steeple rightly, and gives the height of it, but
leaves 2746 (the real Scoat-fell) nameless. The highest peak
after Pillar Fell nameless! But in Bartholomew the title Scoatfell does figure, and prefixed too as a "Great" one; but the name
has slipped south-westwards, and names nothing but a homeless
full stop—a full stop in motion, for it is slipping slowly downwards by the beck which feeds Scoat Tarn. Let us then ask the
truth from the King's Own Majesty . . .

And on consulting the Ordnance Survey map he discovers
that the Queen (as I must bring him up to date), the Queen
calls it "Little" Scoatfell, and the Queen can do no wrong.

I give it up. Personally, I name it Scoatfell, Scoatfell simple
without prefix, suffix, or hesitation. For Scoatfell it is, and its

Gathering Storm, Wastwater

height is 2746, and the Steeple is north of it, and a spur of it, and a very good spur, and is approximately 57 feet lower at its highest point; and that's the end of it.

Ennerdale altogether inspires this writer to one of his best chapters. The passage I have quoted occurs in the account of the eastward facing walk along the ridge from Crag Fell to Pillar Fell, and I know of no finer account or of any finer walk.

Another writer who is at his best on Ennerdale is F. G. Brabant in the delightful volume in *The Little Guides*. He is especially welcome as a companion on the walk round the lake. Anyone who has seen Ennerdale at all has done so either from the remote head of the valley far beyond the lake and looking from Scarth Gap or Black Sail; alternatively it is the view from the Angler's Inn that is photographed on the retina of the eye. If the mountain viewpoint is remote, this view could hardly be closer. The famous old inn stands so close that there is only room to walk past and the water laps beneath the windows in a way of which one could never tire. The situation of the inn is unique. As with Venice one hardly believes until one sees it. For this immediate foreground the mountains provide a noble setting. Ennerdale Water has a strange beauty of its own. It has no islands, and the outlines of the flanking hills are bare, but towards its centre Angling Crag on the right and Bowness Knotts opposite, both beautiful crags, fall from the higher fells and narrow the lake with fine and interesting effect. The river which flows from the lower end is the Ehen, though three miles away the lake is fed by the River Liza which rises on Great Gable. It is an unpredictable lake. The last time I saw it it lay a sheet of blue under a blue sky on a calm windless day in early spring. Then almost without warning a breeze sprang up, blowing from the lower end and increasing at an extraordinary rate to a great force till the surface of the water was broken and choppy and waves with white manes were breaking on the shore. One of the large, flat-bottomed dredgers, which are a reminder that Ennerdale is an important source of water supply for the industrial coast, had been peacefully anchored by the shore, but the wind tore it away from its moorings and sent it revolving in large circles across the surface of the lake, its occupant finding the

Buttermere Lake and Great Gable

motor engine quite inadequate to right it. He was finally carried within reach of a colleague on the opposite shore and pulled to safety.

It is perhaps a matter of temperament whether one is most tempted to sit at the inn and gaze untiringly at the view, or whether one must answer at once the obvious call of the walk round the lake. The path starts off along the north side and for a mile or so is as close to the water's edge as the most venturesome child could wish. On the occasion I have just described the waves were breaking right over the path and my cairn terrier was alternately threatened with either being airborne at any moment or having to swim for it. After a time the path leaves the shore, passes under the crag of Bowness Knotts, and joins the main cart-track, which, running to the left of the River Liza all the way, is obviously the only means of approach along the wild desolate valley that stretches ahead. It is strangely deserted, and in five miles there is no relief except that provided by the solitary farm of Gillerthwaite, and what must be one of the most strategically placed youth hostels in existence. Across the valley the famous giants which Ennerdale claims as its own mountains gradually reveal themselves as we travel up the valley. Pillar Rock is well seen, appearing in face higher than it is in relation to surrounding crags. Green Gable at the head of the valley yields to Great Gable, which shows its steepest ascent. On the left of these is Brandreth and on the right Kirk Fell. The path climbs past the moraine heaps of the Liza valley to Black Sail, the pass which offers an easy bridle path over to Wasdale Head, though it rises to 1,750 feet, and Scarth Gap which climbs to 1,400 feet, and then drops to Buttermere. Pillar, Steeple and Haycock (who suddenly sound like a firm of solicitors), are beloved of adventurous walkers and rock climbers. As viewpoints they have much in common, Pillar being perhaps the best, with its full-length view of Ennerdale Water, part of Loweswater, Burnmoor and Ill Tarns, and a fine array of mountains—Great Gable and the Scafell range, Great End, Grasmoor, Skiddaw and Blencathra, Helvellyn and the Fairfield range. Mosedale valley, which we saw opening out on to the green plain of Wasdale Head, here has its desolate origin at our very feet.

You may return either by the ridge walk to Cragg Fell or
by the side of the lake on the south.

That night at the inn—appropriately in view of its name—
we listened to the anglers denying that the Lakes have a good
supply of fish. In fact there is sufficient even for that great
guzzler the cormorant. The lakes teem with life, from boyhood's conquests, the minnow and stickleback, through perch
and the angler's favourite trout to the beautiful char and the
pike which feeds on them all as well as on moorhens, coots,
or fluffy ducklings stemming in mother's wake, himself having
none to fear but the angler. The char, famous for centuries as
a potted delicacy, lives here as in Windermere and Coniston,
which with Derwentwater and Ullswater are the best of the
larger lakes for the public to fish. Char are caught by the
simple and delightful method of trolling, in which a spinning
bait, red on one side, silver on the other, is used. As a boy
I was assured that nothing came up to the good old practice
of trolling with the backs of gold watches!

It was elsewhere and on another occasion that the theme of
fox-hunting once came up in a memorably informative way,
and indeed it is an appropriate subject almost anywhere in
the Lake District, for besides the Eskdale and Ennerdale
footpack there are also the Melbreak, Blencathra, Coniston
and Ullswater foxhounds—footpacks because, if they are
followed at all, they must be followed on foot. No horse
could follow these packs for far, no horseman in his right
senses would expect his mount to carry him over the roughest
countryside in Britain.

On the occasion I recall, the information was elicited by
an elegant young woman in the bar from two burly figures in
cloth caps, heavy boots, with trousers tucked in their socks
at the top. They had in common a passion for hunting and
she listened with a sort of interested incredulity to their
account of hunts which are certainly sporting occasions
though their primary object is to kill foxes, hunting them
with hounds to a kill which may be on the open moorland of
a fell-top or among the jumbled boulders of a mountain-
side scree; but with no Masters in pink. A glance at the
visitors' book gave me the answer of a kind I had expected
when I saw that she came from Melton Mowbray. She was

impressed when she got out of them that a pack will kill nearly a hundred foxes in a season, but I doubt if she was ever seen among the strenuous foot followers.

Apart from special meets on Bank Holidays, there are seldom big crowds to watch the hunts, and very few people, apart from huntsmen and whips, have the stamina to take them over the tops to be in at the kill. Anything is an excuse for a hunt. An invitation from a sportsman-farmer who provides hospitality for huntsman, whip and hounds, a yell for help from a poultry farmer whose chickens have been stolen in the night, or a report from a dalesman that some lambs are missing will provide a date for the fixture list. Anybody is welcome to attend a hunt, the more the merrier, for no matter how large the crowd they will not hamper the business of the hounds which, more often than not, is done high on the mountains and out of reach of spectators. Out of sight too, often, but occasionally on a sharp, bright winter day, when the air is clearer than the clearest crystal, the watchers below are treated to the sight of the hounds streaming along the fellside, yelping with delight, just a nose behind the fox. The fox is as sure-footed as a chamois, and will sometimes take refuge on a ledge on a sheer crag.

The hounds are not quite so nimble, and the casualty rate among them is high when they try to follow. Or the fox may go to earth among boulders, in which case some scruffy-looking but courageous terriers are entered to try to drive him out. If Reynard's strength is spent he prefers to fight it out underground with the game little dogs, and there's a scuffle, a yapping and growling before the rusty-haired Lakeland terriers emerge triumphant. But sometimes they do not, not because the fox has proved too much for them but because they have followed the fox into an underground labyrinth and cannot find the way out, or the fox may have made its last stand in a spot too narrow for the dog to turn around. Then digging operations start and in some cases hundreds of tons of rock have been moved to liberate a terrier, in operations which have extended over a week. There are places where for this reason terriers are not sent in after foxes, and there the foxes are left to run another day—the only occasions when the Lakeland footpacks do not hunt to the kill.

How little Lakeland can afford to allow a fox a "life" is seen in the fact that the vermin are so numerous that often when one fox is being hunted another is put up, and another and another, especially when the original fox heads into the forestry plantations which provide cover, and the result is that these Lakeland packs are often divided, with three or even four hunts going on at once, sometimes only a pair of hounds coursing the quarry. With these multiple hunts it is sometimes difficult to say whether the hounds have killed or not at the end of the day, but the unwritten law is that the carcass of the fox must be seen, or "picked", before a kill is registered—unless there is an undoubted kill underground. In the fells and the western foothills the hunting season is a long one. The end comes after lambing time. The Herdwick lambs and the fox cubs come at the same time, and the cubs must be fed. Slaughter among the lambs brings out the footpacks thirsting for vengeance—and there is no quarter, even the fox cubs being killed where they are found. And when the hunting season finishes at the end of April the hounds go for their holidays in summer quarters, living with farmers who are supporters of the hunt, growing fat but never lazy, for they will hunt foxes on their own if they find them when they go out for their exercise.

The dalesmen who follow the traditions of John Peel, the blood of whose foxhounds still runs in the Blencathra Pack, are born to sport and hunt. Behind them are centuries of hunting going back to the days when a hunt meant the stopping of the day's work, gathering in a pack of "hounds" of almost every known breed of dog and killing the vermin which threatened their livestock. Then perhaps as now, the best part of the hunt was the end of it, for the phrase "hungry as hunters" describes something real, and what better to satisfy such appetites than "tatie-pots" made in huge dishes with the meat of the Herdwicks, and a large black pudden on top? Today a hunt supper's main dish is still tatie-pot, and ale is the main drink, and the hunting songs which tell the stories of the great hunts of bygone days are still sung, there being such a repertoire of these that the singing goes on long after the licensee has called "Time, gentlemen, please!"

CHAPTER VIII

Buttermere, Crummock and Loweswater

To motor from Ennerdale to the valley of the three lakes Buttermere, Crummock Water and Loweswater you must follow the twisty roads through Ennerdale Bridge, the scene of Wordsworth's pastoral poem *The Brothers*, and Lamplugh. You will then have the advantage of approaching the valley from its tamer, lower end and realising how the three lakes depend upon each other's beauty for their full effect. This is the case, however, from whatever point of view they are seen, and the walker, once he has climbed out of Ennerdale's enclosing wall has a choice of several approaches. From the Angler's Inn he can go by Floutern (flow-tarn, the tarn of the bog) over the moors to Scale Force or Mosedale. Alternatively there is a path from lonely Gillerthwaite up Red Pike, but the classic walk is the one from which we turned away at Scarth Gap. It in turn reaches Red Pike over the ridge of High Stile. From Red Pike you not only have a splendid view of the three lakes but an interesting contrast among the kinds of scenery resulting from three different geological formations. To the north and north-east is Skiddaw slate, to the west and south is the grey crystalline syenite and in between them Eskdale granite. You may, however, have approached from Borrowdale, in which case your first impression from Honister Hause at the head of the valley will be of the austere, secluded beauty of Buttermere, again enhanced by the softer charms of Crummock and gentle Loweswater. From the summit of the pass the top of Honister Crag is not a difficult conquest. The Crag is really a part of the mountain Fleetwith, and inside half an hour you can walk to the top which

123

*Looking south-south-west down
the Buttermere Valley*

commands its own view of the three lakes with High Stile,
Red Pike and Melbreak on the left and Robinson and
Grasmoor on the right. Great Gable and the Pillar dominate
the view to the south.

Fortunately the beauty of Buttermere is now safely in the
hands of the National Trust. In relation to its valley, the
lake displays characteristics opposite to those of Ennerdale
Water. When from its mountain head you look down the
latter, a long narrow valley terminates in the lake, giving an
impression that there is the escape to the sea. Buttermere,
on the other hand, is thrust right into the head of the valley
so that the mountains look down on it at the top and on both
sides, and the way of escape lies past two other lakes before
the mind's eye can fly out to the open and the Solway Firth.
Perhaps that way of expressing it shows in itself a dis-
inclination to be too hemmed in by mountains, and I must
own to a mild claustrophobia in Buttermere though I re-visit
it with endless delight in its beauty. The situation of the
Scale Hill Hotel commanding the romantic valley and the
outward prospect seems to me ideal.

Buttermere offers many delightful little walks close to the
village, such as that to Rannerdale or the fine waterfall of
Scale Force. The succession of little cataracts that drop into
the north-west corner of the lake is Sour Milk Gill, a name
which seems ideal for many similar falls in other parts. The
stretch of flat land which separates Buttermere and Crummock is memorable for me for the recollection of the first
wild fox I ever saw loping across through the grass. The
last got up in front of me near Dalegarth Farm, slinking
over the nearest rocks from what I can only think was a
disturbed afternoon's sleep. But there is no finer valley for
the study of wild life in the Lake District than the one we
are now in. It endlessly renews the interest in striking
contrast to the story of Mary of Buttermere, whose marital
misfortunes have provided far too much copy for the Lake
poets and the scratch-pot hacks who have followed them.

We all tend to identify the wild life with those parts of
the district in which we have had fortunate glimpses as I
did of my fox between Buttermere and Crummock. Although
I seem always to have had my best views of buzzards high

The summit of Honister Pass ➤

over the crags at the back of Skiddaw and Saddleback, there
are many of them, particularly in the Loweswater district,
great golden-brown birds with wing-tip feathers outspread
like the fingers of a hand. They can wheel for hours in the
sky without beating their wings, swinging slowly in circles,
mewing plaintively or, like the last pair I watched, feeding
by the fascinating method whereby in the threading arabesque
in the sky the female turns on her back to receive what her
mate has brought her. It may be a grim offering but unlike
the raven which will peck out the eyes of a dying sheep or
one that has managed to thrust its head out of a snow-drift,
the buzzard does wait till its prey is dead, and as a scavenger
performs a useful task cleaning up the remains of sheep
which die on the fells, and which would otherwise pollute the
water supplies which Cumberland towns take from the lakes.
Buzzards also help in keeping down the numbers of rabbits.
They nest either in large trees or, eagle-like, on the crags.

There are fewer ravens, but the almost-musical "cronk"
which they make as they go about their business is a sociable
sound in summer, even if it sounds ominous in winter. An
old raven nest, one that has been in occupation for many
years, contains a wagon-load of sticks, and the biggest is
undoubtedly that on Great Borne at the head of the Loweswater Mosedale. This nest is inaccessible, and the same pair
of ravens has used it perhaps for a century. The peregrine
falcon is denied protection these days, a hangover from the
war years when it was said it preyed on carrier pigeons.
Possibly, but it also takes toll of wood pigeons, and can dive
at a hundred miles an hour, strike the head off a pigeon, and
carry the body in triumph to the nest on a ledge up the crags.
Kestrels also nest on the crags, and sparrow-hawks are found
in the woods, but the little merlin, most beautiful of all
hawks, is found only on the open moorlands, laying its eggs
among the heather stalks a few yards from its "killing stone",
a rock where all its prey—mostly small birds—is dressed
before being fed to the young. The curlew is another bird of
the mountain-top, and there also may still be found the rare
dotterel. In the gullies nests the ring-ouzel, that white-
collared blackbird, and in the jumbled stones of the screes
are the wheatears whose "song" is like the noise made when

stones are knocked together. In May of this year 1954, golden eagles were reported. They are already back in Dumfries as nesting birds and may well grace the fells and crags again.

In most of the valleys there is a variety of birds which includes practically every resident and immigrant species found in England. One variety, the green woodpecker, has recently returned to the district and is increasing, and the corncrake is now heard more often than it was before the war. But the little bird that is the very symbol of the Lake District is a black and white beauty, the pied flycatcher, of which there are more here than in any other part of the country.

Where there are lakes, there are naturally many water birds, and a few hours at Loweswater will reveal the great crested grebe, a variety of duck, coots, waterhens, and cormorants.

My friend Mr. Carruthers, who is able to combine in the happiest way newspaper editing and nature study, has always some new discovery to report. Though I have never seen one, there are apparently many badgers, but these big ungainly fellows only go out at night, and spend their days sleeping in their setts, large underground defences which grow with the family. The Lake District is probably the one place in England where the pine marten lives. This is a cousin of the polecat, and because its smell is not so objectionable, is called the "sweet mart". Chocolate-brown in colour, with creamy breast, it lives in the forestry plantations in safety, but in very small numbers, for it was believed a few years ago to have become extinct. Today it can be found, but only by chance, because it is the shyest of animals. Incidentally red deer, always to be found over on the far side of the district in Martindale, have increased and spread lately through Westmorland right down to the valley of the Lune.

There is apparently only one dangerous creature—the adder—and one can come across it on hot days sunning itself on a stone in that "lost world" of Burnmoor where we saw the stone circles of a forgotten civilization dotting the landscape.

When I asked Mr. Carruthers which part the student of natural history would find most interesting he replied:

The whole of the area teems with wild life, but to choose three areas where the biggest variety is to be found, I would say Holme Wood, Loweswater, for the birds of lake and wood-land. For birds of the mountains—raven, buzzard, peregrine, kestrel, wheatear, and ring-ouzel—Melbreak mountain is the place, and for moorland life there is Burnmoor between Eskdale and Wasdale.

Loweswater lies in its own valley which turns to the north-west. The River Cocker, issuing from Crummock Water, flows north through the Vale of Lorton of which Miss Doreen Wallace, who had the good fortune to spend her childhood there, writes so delightfully. It would be hard to turn to the countryside of which Keswick is the centre without first looking at Cockermouth, which waits only a few miles ahead at the confluence with the Derwent. You can see the house in which Wordsworth was born though the place did not seem to influence him much. It is a schoolmate whose story provides the dominating interest.

We have already seen how Curwens, Christians, Fletchers and their connections run through all the history of the district. At Moorland Close, three miles from Cockermouth, was born Fletcher Christian, the leader of the mutiny on the *Bounty*.

The lane leading from Moorland Close enters the main street of Cockermouth immediately opposite the birthplace of Wordsworth; the poet and Fletcher Christian were fellow-pupils at Cockermouth Grammar School, and the fact is commemorated by a plaque on the site of the old school. (On this plaque the date of the mutiny is incorrectly given as 1788.) But in a recent book of hugely entertaining and ingenious detective-work, Mr. C. S. Wilkinson builds up, slender hint by hint, the fascinating theory that there was a later and more intimate connection between mutineer and poet. Many men have believed that Fletcher Christian did not die on Pitcairn but managed to find his way back to England. The accounts of his death given by the one surviving mutineer to visiting ships are oddly—and so perhaps deliberately—misleading. Sir John Barrow, writing in 1831, gives the story of how Heywood, a midshipman mutineer condemned but pardoned at the *Bounty* court-martial, saw in Plymouth, about 1808 or 1809, an elusive figure which he was sure was Christian; and there were in the Lake District at this time strong rumours of Christian's presence. Mr. Wilkinson first caught the scent of his trail by finding in a second-hand bookshop a letter signed "F. Christian" and dated 1812.

If Fletcher Christian returned secretly to England, he would presumably have been sure of help from his important social and political connections. Already in 1794, indeed, his brother Edward, a predecessor of Wordsworth's at St. John's, Cambridge, and his headmaster at Hawkshead Grammar School, had published a vindication of Fletcher. Edward's method had been to interview and take statements from available participants in the mutiny. The witnesses to these interviews, as Mr. Wilkinson points out, included Wordsworth's uncle, Canon Cookson, his cousin, Captain John Wordsworth, his college tutor, Dr. Frewen, and his friends Losh, Gilpin and Antrobus. It is almost astounding, in view of all these direct and indirect connections, personal and local, between Fletcher Christian and William Wordsworth, that there is no mention whatsoever, in all the published correspondence of William and Dorothy Wordsworth, of either the *Bounty* or its chief mutineer. Was Wordsworth deliberately reticent about the *Bounty*, as he was so successfully about Annette Vallon until pitiless modern scholarship floodlit the episode? Mr. Wilkinson, weaving his slender threads of evidence, believes that some time in 1795 (nine months of which year is a total blank in Wordsworth's biography) Wordsworth met Fletcher Christian in Bristol, hid him briefly in Nether Stowey (whose rector was an intimate friend of the Law family), and finally smuggled him safely away to other of the ubiquitous Christian connections, probably in Dumfries-shire. During this misty period in the poet's life he first met Coleridge, and in Nether Stowey the two friends would have been able to hear from Fletcher Christian:

> How a ship having passed the line was driven
> by storms to the cold country towards the South
> Pole; and how from thence she made her course
> to the tropical latitude of the great Pacific
> ocean; and of the strange things that befell;
> and in what manner the ancyent marinere came back
> to his own country.

Mr. Wilkinson claims this preface to the early *Lyrical Ballads* version of Coleridge's masterpiece as "an accurate summary of the story of the *Bounty* and Fletcher Christian". He can adduce in support a mysterious line from Coleridge's note-books for the period 1795–8: "Adventures of *Christian* the Mutineer", as a possible topic for a poem. Coleridge and de Quincey tell a story of how a spy was sent down to Nether Stowey apparently to investigate the two poets' Francophile tendencies. Mr. Wilkinson has a theory about him, too: it was Captain Bligh himself, on the look-out for his old antagonist, and the reason the spy's reports are missing from the Home Office files is that they were removed by the Duke of Portland, an ally of the Christian family.

"The *Bounty* story", says Mr. David Curnow, "is full of the Zeitgeist of the Romantic Age. It was a small-scale revolution and it took place, with a beautiful appropriateness, in the year of the greatest of all revolutions, 1789. One cause of the mutiny was the attractions of the simple and natural life of the South Seas and the charms of the Otaheitan women. The Romantic 'back to Nature', the cult of 'the noble savage', the passion for the founding of new societies like Coleridge's scheme for a colony on the banks of the Susquehanna—some of the dearest Romantic dreams were briefly given shape on Pitcairn, however far from Utopian the results turned out to be. The one survivor of the mutineers on Pitcairn, Alexander Smith, was discovered by the *Topaz* piously bringing up the children of his dead comrades, but now naming himself a patriarchal John Adams —a fine deliberate touch of art in this remarkable fable." Whether or not we can accept Mr. Wilkinson's theories as historically true, it is at least artistically appropriate that the chief actor in the Romantic mutiny should have been involved with the greatest poet of the Romantic Age.

CHAPTER IX

Bassenthwaite

BASSENTHWAITE has a beauty and interest which by comparison with the assault made by other lakes are insinuating. They are, however, very real, and though at first one thinks that Bassenthwaite is adequately acknowledged as a feature in the diminishing perspective of many splendid views from the mountain-tops of Borrowdale and elsewhere, it establishes in later years with those who give it the opportunity a firm hold on the affections. It lies between Cockermouth and Keswick and points the way out to the sea. Indeed, the Castle Hotel at the northern end is one of those farewell points which mark definitely the perimeter of the Lake District. Among others similarly situated are The Sun at Pooley Bridge, The Swan at Newby Bridge, The Anglers' Inn on Ennerdale Water. The western shore commands splendid views of Skiddaw and Saddleback and they in turn look across the lake to a wonderful panorama of mountains. Skiddaw, of course, has always been a favourite of the poets and many a fine line in the Arthur poems seems to reflect the holiday that in 1835 Tennyson and Fitzgerald spent at Mirehouse on Bassenthwaite with James Spedding, the Baconian.

> On one side lay the ocean, and on one
> Lay a great water, and the moon was full.

On such nights the two young men would push off from the shore and from their boat hear "the long ripple washing in the reeds", or perhaps imagine that they saw Excalibur "the sword that rose from out the bosom of the lake." Canon Rawnsley, who depicts the scene imaginatively, points out how thick upon the ground were poet laureates in these earlier years of the nineteenth century—Southey, Wordsworth,

Tennyson—and he paints a charming vignette of the scene in October, 1850, outside Miss Robson's millinery shop in Keswick where Alfred Tennyson, a fine gypsy-looking man, and his dainty bride might have been observed in conversation with Miss Spedding in the open Mirehouse carriage. Tennyson, without disclosing his identity, made courteous inquiries after his friend James Spedding and was invited with his wife to take seats in the carriage and pay a call at Mirehouse. For nearly four miles Miss Spedding was left wondering who this "fine-featured, dim-eyed, bronze-coloured, shaggy-headed man is; dusty, smoking, free and easy". Only at the gates did he announce with grim humour, "I am Alfred Tennyson, James's friend, and this, madam, is my wife". Their arrival caused a great stir in the quiet house, but everything was noted by a little girl who many years later described it all to Canon Rawnsley just as others told him of Carlyle's visit to the house in 1865 and with so much first-hand information the Canon wrote one of his most evocative chapters about the literary associations with this lake. In the jackdaw-like process of snapping up other people's good things I will turn, however, to Miss Doreen Wallace, who is the only source I know for a story which, as she says, has a strange Thomas Hardy-like quality, and which she tells in *English Lakeland*. The scene was at Ouse Bridge,

> a pretty dell with a river which offers good fishing.... A young man came courting a farmer's daughter, and courted too closely: she pressed him to marry her, and he said he would, but, said he, since his parents were against it, it would have to be a Gretna wedding. He made arrangements to meet her, with a horse, by night on the bridge. She came to the tryst—and under pretence of mounting her on the horse, he lifted her and flung her over the bridge's low parapet. How he must have hated her for trapping him: what a fear inspired that desperate and brutal plan!
>
> She was carrying, however, a parasol; and it opened with the fall and kept her up (that is the story, but maybe her ballooning skirts saved her, or perhaps she could swim). At all events, he beheld her next day, risen from her watery grave and come to lay the story before the uncle, with whom he worked. The uncle felled him to earth with a dung-fork. The lad was committed to the Assizes, but died of cholera before his case

could be heard. The story was written up as a novel about seventy years ago by one Thomas Thorpe, of Cockermouth, but only privately circulated; the date of the event was about 1836.

The vagaries of literary fame are strangely unpredictable. This farmer's daughter has remained comparatively unknown, whilst her sister in misfortune, Mary of Buttermere, has been written to death. Similarly, the village of Caldbeck, back of Skiddaw, was the home of John Peel, who died a hundred years ago. His renown as a huntsman is not only local but stretches to every quarter of the globe. When John Woodcock Graves, a woollen weaver of Caldbeck, sat by the fire with John Peel in 1832 and composed the words to a tune of which the rhythm was inspired by an old rant called Bonny Annie which was being sung at the time by an old woman crooning one of Graves' children to sleep, they could not conceivably have foreseen the extraordinary and enduring fame that still survives, a hundred years after his death, of this local huntsman. A strange adhesiveness mysteriously attaches in this way to the occasional item among all those which the process of cultural diffusion is forever spreading. For instance, among the items that process brought to this remote hill village have been immigrant miners, ice-cream vendors, post-cards (aesthetic as Sir Evelyn Wrench intended when he introduced them into this country fifty years ago, or vulgar, unconsciously enshrining sociological values which George Orwell so brilliantly analysed) and many other things amongst them the names of the news readers of the B.B.C. which were heard, during the war associated with epoch-making events of world importance. Will one of those names be known on this hill-side a hundred years hence?

Another bone which I must leave the professional philosophers to chew over is: at what point in the long process between Skiddaw's lying beneath the waters of the timeless sea and its famous domination of the poets did beauty emerge? We must leave it to the philosophers who can indulge in abstract speculation because we are involved in the practical problem of getting along, and also because, given that beauty has emerged, no one can have had a more tricky question to decide as guardians of it than we in our

day, confronted with the problem of afforestation in the Lake District. Even in such an area as this much of the most beautiful scenery is man-made. It has been suggested that the moment of perfect co-operation passed with the farm-houses and stone walls of the seventeenth and eighteenth centuries. But never has man changed the face of nature so extensively as have the activities of the Forestry Commission, and we have each a responsibility as individuals to assess the opposing cases.

As I write, the defenders of the Lake District, eternally vigilant, are reaching for their pens again to deal with the reported intentions of the Forestry Commission. Like Birnam itself, the Commissioners on the move present a spectacle likely to create the deepest dismay and arouse the most melancholy forebodings. This time, alarm has been caused by rumours, reports and suspicions that the Commissioners want to tamper with the 1936 Agreement, which is holy writ, setting down as it does the terms of the armistice signed by the Commission and the Council for the Preservation of Rural England. That armistice marked the end of a long and vehement struggle in which many of the most exalted in the land fought to retain the essential character of the Lake District against what they held to be the threat from the Forestry Commission.

One of the earliest of the State forests had already been planted on either side of Bassenthwaite Lake. It now consists of 5,000 acres divided into plantations lying north, south, east and west of the lake. The first slice of land to be acquired by the Commission in this part of the Lake District took in over 1,100 acres around Whinlatter Pass. And of the scene at Whinlatter as it has been transformed by the Commissioners, the Rev. H. H. Symonds, that particularly ferocious friend of the Lake District, has written in a paragraph that expresses much of the objection to commercial afforestation such as the Commissioners engage in.

> The planting is continuous, by the square mile. Where there was colour, this is first hidden, then dissolved. . . . What is seen is the rigid and monotonous ranks of spruce, dark green to blackish, goose-stepping on the fell side. Their colour—you must except the larch—is in effect one steady tone all round

Looking north-north-east from
the Vale of St. John

the dull year; there are no glories of spring and autumn for the conifer. Sunlight, which a broad-leaved, deciduous tree reflects and vivifies, is annihilated on their absorbent texture; on a bright landscape they are so much blotting paper. Bird life perishes, for there are no berried trees, as plant life perishes. The barren undergrowth of a coniferous woodland is a pale, bloodless thing. And to the long, unbroken mileage of drab, dead colour, with the Sitka spruce king of this gloomy kingdom, you must add the curse of uniformity in growth. For conifers are patterned trees, branching evenly and subservient to arboreal geometry.

This violent stirring amid the coniferous forest does not imply a downright denunciation of all commercial afforestation everywhere. In this century, and especially towards the middle of the century, the glory of the trees and their goodness, the contribution they make to man's welfare, have been rediscovered. The evil consequences of the denuding of our forest land—soil erosion and all that that means in loss of fertility—are widely preached, and hence more widely acknowledged. The wisdom of the ancient days is recalled with sighs of envy. We have been reminded that Plato spoke of the sickening of his country caused by the clearance of forests and that Cicero, in his Second Phillipic, condemned the destroyers of forests as enemies of the public weal. Nearer home and nearer our own time, the seed of State action to put things to rights began to sprout half a century ago when, after a series of inconclusive inquiries, reports and commissions, the Development Commission was authorized to turn some of its attention to forestry and experimental areas began to be acquired. A fuller story of the germination has been given by Mr. W. L. Taylor, one-time Assistant Forestry Commissioner for England and Wales, in his *Forests and Forestry in Great Britain*. The Forestry Commission, set up by Act of Parliament in 1919, is charged with the general duty of promoting the interests of forestry, the development of afforestation, and the production and supply of timber in Great Britain. In the years when unemployment fell as a blight on the land, the importance of afforestation in providing work was much emphasized. Indeed, in a pamphlet put out only a year or two ago, in the era of full

employment, the Commissioners referred with some pride
to the fact that Thornthwaite gives employment to nearly
one hundred men. The case for growing more of the timber
we need at home was put with effect (even before the dollar
gap began to yawn) by Mr. Taylor in the book already
referred to. In the years before the Second World War, only
four per cent of the country's requirements were met from
home woodlands, and as much as £120,000,000 was paid to
foreign suppliers in a single year. None of this is challenged.

> No criticism is implied [wrote Mr. Symonds in his *Afforestation
> in the Lake District*] of the wisdom of setting up such a body or
> of the Commissioners' general policy; these wider considerations
> do not arise. In any case, it is clear that the production of
> timber is a needful part of good agriculture and also that it
> may be, in various ways, a means of rural beauty.

The protests have rested on three bastions: against woodland
that is exclusively coniferous, against continuous plantation
that blankets all the natural diversity and interferes with
public access, and against lower-level planting with its en-
croachment on Herdwick sheep farming. In some places,
where the mountains are higher and the proportions very
different, conifers, faster growing and more profitable than
the broad-leaved trees, may be acceptable; but the Lake
District is held as a special case because of its intense con-
centration and variety. On the subject of public access,
Mr. Symonds has covered the ground with familiar gusto:

> Once the Commissioners have bought and therefore have
> necessarily fenced, the best that can be done is to secure
> continued access to these plantations by certain recognized
> and canalized pathways. . . . Like all others who know and love
> the district, I abominate this regimentation and cross-gartering
> of tracks and hanker for the old-fashioned, skimble-skamble,
> bandy-legged divergencies which took us as the spirit moved
> or the slope invited. I lack the proper mentality to enjoy some
> enlarged and interminable Southport Flower Show, with all the
> visitors kindly requested to keep on the proper pathways.

The growth of the Thornthwaite estate at Whinlatter
involved the displacement of four flocks of Herdwicks—1,600
head of sheep in all—an example of what the protestants

mean when they deplore the sentence that afforestation imposes on the Herdwicks, valuable, as they have averred, for both their wool and their mutton. But in its own defence the Commission has pointed out, in dealing with Thornthwaite for instance, that part of the land at Darling How is reserved for sheep farming and carries a flock of Herdwicks and that the present rate of employment at Thornthwaite, one man to 35 acres, "contrasts strongly with the position when the bare land was taken over only thirty years ago. At that time only a very few shepherds and gamekeepers were employed over the same area." Whether the finding of employment holds the importance now that it did between the wars impinges upon economics, and so does the debate on whether in the long run afforestation will be a paying proposition in an area of such special difficulty as the Lake District.

But wounds opened up by these and other issues looked much less angry when the tourniquet of 1936 was applied. By the agreement reached between the Forestry Commission and the Council for the Preservation of Rural England, the Commissioners undertook "to refrain voluntarily from acquiring land within an area of about 300 square miles in the centre of the Lake District". They acknowledged that this area, by reason of its unusual beauty and seclusion and its remoteness, should be ruled out altogether from afforestation by the Commissioners. On a map accompanying the agreement, however, an area in the south and south-west of the Lake District was shaded. About the future of this area the Commissioners could give no clear-cut promise, despite all the persuasions of the C.P.R.E.

For nearly twenty years, the "Magna Carta" as it has been called, has stood inviolate. "For how long more?" ask the Lake District friends, for they see large nimbus clouds floating up over the fells. The Forestry Act of 1951 pays special attention to the statutory duty of the Forestry Commission to ensure maintenance of private woodlands in a healthy condition, and it is now known that the Commission is seeking amendment of the 1936 Agreement so that it may acquire or lease private woodlands anywhere in the Lake District. "Delicate" negotiations with the C.P.R.E.

are in progress. But much worse news than that has slipped
out. From a source of high integrity it is reported that for
one awful moment the Commission declared the 1936 agreement no longer in force. That is enough to send the defenders
scampering out to the ramparts again ready with all their
heavy cannon to fight against the upward and onward march
of the conifer.

CHAPTER X

Keswick, Derwentwater and Borrowdale

KESWICK is an excellent centre and has many amenities for the tourist, but apart from the lawns of Fitz
Park immediately outside the station, it is unattrac-
tive in itself and strangely affords no glimpse of the beauty of
the scenery by which it is immediately surrounded. The one
main street is relieved by the Town Hall, which strikes a
curiously foreign note in the middle of the market place.
Otherwise the shop fronts and hotels are aggressively un-
picturesque. You can stand and watch the activity of the open
market on a Saturday. Only the flowers and the plants seem
to enjoy the rain. In every window into which you glance
eating is in earnest progress. The scene seems to get busier
and busier until you suddenly notice that you are almost
overwhelmed by a preponderance either of clergymen or
women with an indefinable air in common and you realise
that Keswick must be fulfilling one of its particular functions,
which is to house conferences and conventions of various
kinds. The liveliness makes it tolerable, but a rainy Sunday
afternoon in Keswick can touch a considerable depth of dreariness. Then you seem to be able only to get into the shabbier
and culpably unenterprising cafes. The smell of fish and
chips fills the air at four o'clock in the afternoon. Ice cream
and tomato ketchup stand side by side on the stained table-
cloth. The eye seems to rest on nothing but steaming coats,
bicycles, babies—"Whatever's written in . . . the book of the
people." It elevates no rhyme.

Yet this is above all others the town of poets. Here Shelley
brought his bride for their honeymoon, as did Coleridge,
Southey and John Ruskin. Wordsworth, de Quincey and

Charles Lamb all have associations with the place, and Greta
Hall, which one can see from the road after crossing the
bridge at the bottom of the main street, must have some claim
to be considered the house of all others in England with the
richest literary associations. Its story was told by Mr. H. W.
Howe, the headmaster of Keswick School of which the house
now forms a part, in a little book of which only 500
copies were privately printed, in 1943. It is a book that
deserves to be more widely known. Coleridge and Southey,
the sisters they married, and their children, their visitors and
friends, people the rooms with the actuality of the furniture
and the views from the windows. Lamb, Hazlitt, de Quincey,
Wordsworth and Shelley are only the most outstanding of
other names in the annals of Greta Hall. It was a notable
domestic event and a charming curiosity in English literature
when, in September 1829, Sara was married to her cousin,
Henry Nelson Coleridge. The son of Wordsworth performed
the ceremony at Crosthwaite; her "father-uncle" Southey
gave her away, the three Southey cousins and Dorothy
Wordsworth were among the bridesmaids. The visitors'
book yields many interesting names: James Boswell junr.,
William Wilberforce, Walter Savage Landor, Walter Scott,
the poet Rogers, Lockhart, Barry Cornwall, Dr. Arnold,
Crabb Robinson, the reformer Clarkson, Canning, Robert
Owen, Humphry Davy, John Stuart Mill—I have space to
mention only those that immediately catch the eye, and no
room for the impressive list of books that were produced in
this house. Mr. Howe concludes:

> The story ends as it begins, with "Only the voice of the Greta
> heard only when all else is stillness" and the cawing of the rooks
> in the beech trees, and perhaps the crackling of a fire in
> Coleridge's study, "the low voice of quiet change, doing its
> work by little and little"; but never completing its work.

The parish church for Keswick is at Crosthwaite, nearly a
mile from the centre of the town. This is one of the oldest and
most interesting churches in the Lake District. It is a very
ancient foundation dedicated to St. Kentigern, the Bishop of
Glasgow, who was almost certainly here in the sixth century,
and is more familiarly known as St. Mungo. Here too we may

reverence the memory of Canon and Mrs. Rawnsley. The Canon, who was vicar of the parish for thirty-four years and is commemorated in the Baptistry, was one of the earliest and remains one of the greatest of the benefactors who have enabled the National Trust to acquire so much property in the district on behalf of the public. If I may direct attention to what in my opinion would be the most attractive spot in the Lake District at which to live, I recommend the road that leads on beyond Crosthwaite to Applethwaite. It was Southey's opinion that the terrace between Applethwaite and Millbeck, the next village about a mile on, gave the best general view of Derwentwater. I would put its claim higher, and even from what one can see of the houses from outside I should imagine Applethwaite is a little hamlet of connoisseurs. The situation certainly ought to inspire an architect and stay the hand of the vandal. From under the sheltering side of Skiddaw one looks across a mile or two of meadow foreground through which the River Derwent flows from its own lake into Bassenthwaite. The two lakes, it is clear, were originally one, but the intervening stretch of land, like that between Crummock and Buttermere, has been created by the streams flowing towards each other from either side flooding and silting up. The principal contributors in this case through countless centuries have been the River Greta flowing down from under Saddleback, and Newlands Beck from the valley of that name. As a feature of the picturesque scene it provides an example of how opinions may differ and cannot profitably be disputed. Baddeley thinks Southey's opinion cannot be sustained because the foreground is not strong enough to support the exceptional beauty of the other parts of the picture. To my mind the mountain panorama is just at the distance at which I like mountains to be, and the view is greatly enriched by the foreground, flat and fertile. To the right, Bassenthwaite leads off in what is so clearly the direction of the sea that one feels no oppression from the mountains. The prospect includes practically all the features visible from the more famous viewpoint of Castle Head on the shore of Derwentwater. Applethwaite has the advantage of being sufficiently back and above the valley as to command the greatest length of Borrowdale, Derwentwater and

Bassenthwaite, the first length of which appears on the right. Beginning at this point we see just above the end of the lake the steep screes of Barf, among them a strangely formed piece of rock, which from time to time is whitewashed, and which is known as the Bishop of Barf. Next comes Lord's Seat and then the easily recognized depression of Whinlatter Pass, which brings the road over from Cockermouth through the picturesquely situated little village of Braithwaite, in many ways the ideal spot from which to explore most of the northern lakes. The pass has come down under the shoulder of Grisedale Pike, the next prominent mountain. It is one that rewards the climber with good views, but the last stretch to the summit, not unlike Striding Edge in formation, is dangerous and exhausting. Barrow, nearer to us, is Braithwaite's own domestic hill. Immediately behind it, after the straight ridge. of Ill Crag and Sail, Causey Pike rises in characteristic outline. This is one of the mountains with such individual crests that once memorized they greatly help in identifying other mountains, although, of course, everything is changed according to the point of the compass from which one sees them. The next and much more distant mountains are those that stand around Buttermere, Red Pike, High Stile and a little nearer and bulking more prominently, Robinson. Then in the foreground and rising from Derwentwater itself is Catbells, another outline almost unmistakable once known. One can make out the direction of the wonderful ridge walk which continues over Maiden Moor high above Borrowdale, along the other Eel Crags behind Scawdel Fell (glorious this energetic and not too exhausting elevation between Borrowdale and Newlands valley) to Dale Head and Robinson with Honister Pass down below leading to all the joys of Buttermere. These cannot be seen from our present viewpoint but they can be resolved upon. Scawdel Fell is nearly seven miles distant. To the left of it and another six miles beyond is Scafell Pike, with Black Crag and Great End, and rising from the lake in the foreground to this Castle Crag, and on the same plain Brund Fell just across the (from here) invisible River Derwent. Back on the skyline are Esk Pike and Glaramara, and in the foreground the wooded crags of Ashness Fells that hang above Lodore.

It was up the back of the hill called Catbells that, without waiting for thanks or the washing bill, Mrs. Tiggy-Winkle was last seen running, running, running, till she disappeared into a door; and because, most oddly, nothing could be seen of her white frilled cap, her shawl, her gown and her petticoat, and because she seemed to have grown so small and brown and be covered with prickles, little Lucie of Newlands got the impression that Mrs. Tiggy-Winkle was nothing but a hedgehog. Still, as Beatrix Potter said afterwards, she knew that door and was very well acquainted with dear Mrs. T. and how else could Lucie have found "three clean pocket-handkies and a pinny, pinned with a silver safety-pin?"

It is an appropriate recollection with which to embark on the exploration of the idyllic Vale of Newlands—remote and pretty and in utter contrast to the wild joys of Borrowdale from which it is divided by the range that runs down to Catbells and leads Newlands towards Bassenthwaite. At the head of the valley are three branches, each with its own beck. The East or main branch is nearest to Borrowdale and ends in Dale Head—a remote, deep-set valley well worth exploring. Hindscarth divides it from Little Dale, the middle branch. Then comes Robinson and the Keskadale branch, up which Buttermere Hause climbs and descends to Buttermere village. The dark crags at this end of the vale are in striking contrast to the pastoral beauty of the parts nearer Bassenthwaite.

This year, after a long and wonderful spring, the approach of June was marked by one of those freakish cold spells that are not uncommon, and the hills were unexpectedly covered with snow. During the next day or two the summer again established itself and the result in Newlands was quite enchanting. I followed the beck past the little old manor house through meadows that suddenly seemed more lush and green than ever. In one, a sleek and solitary foal, in another a flock of sheep peacefully cropping, the block of firs and larches on the hill-side, with green beeches among the dark trees, the air full of the sound of birds and water, and the blossom of the hawthorn and the bird-cherry repeating the white of the mountain-tops were unforgettable. This was winter's last little fling, and I can remember other years when it has been dramatically dismissed; one in particular, when

The Landing Stage hard by
Friars Crag, Derwentwater

Buttermere lake was almost indistinguishable from the pelting downpour of rain to which at the top of Honister was added cloud and then whirling snow settling incongruously on the green leaves that were already out. We almost groped our way down to lunch in Borrowdale, and when we stepped out an hour later it was as though over Honister great doors had swung to, implacably shutting the winter out whilst the spring sunshine in Borrowdale shone on the mountain-tops and gleamed in every pool and raindrop. Most memorable on that occasion was the snowy aspect with which Skiddaw looked down on Derwentwater as we journeyed north.

There is no gainsaying those for whom Derwentwater is the most beautiful of the lakes. They are not to be moved, and it is but waste of breath, for Derwentwater with its beautiful shape, rich surrounding scenery, trim wooded islands and noble mountain background is lovely beyond argument. The strenuous pleasures of Borrowdale lie ahead. They always begin, I feel, at Grange. Before then there is much immediate beauty to enjoy in return for little exertion. The twelve miles round the lake by road yield splendid views. Castle Head is a famous point for an overall view, Friars Crag for one which though less extensive is right on the lake. There are boat trips from which a closer view of the islands may be obtained. The three larger ones are Derwent Isle which is private property near the landings, Lord's Island, now National Trust, and St. Herbert's Island in the middle of the lake where Herebert, the disciple of St. Cuthbert, lived in the seventh century. Between here and the eastern shore the National Trust own the small island of Rampsholme and what is marked on the map as Floating Island, near Lodore, appears very occasionally, caused by marsh gas which bears to the surface a tangled mass of vegetation and growing plants. The east side of the lake is the most rewarding with which to begin. On this side are Walla Crag and the famous Falls of Lodore, but the finest walk is to Watendlath, a famously remote tarn with a couple of farms high up in the middle of the block of moorland that divides Borrowdale from Thirlmere. It is fascinating in itself, but the great charm of the excursion lies in the views from the hill as you climb from Derwentwater. There are beautiful woods above Lodore and splendid views of Borrowdale from the fell track between Watendlath and Rosthwaite. Indeed it gets a Baddeley superlative—"It is perhaps the most glorious valley-view in Britain." Nowhere else in fact is so peppered with this equivalent of Baedeker's four stars as this valley and though he may have to be rationed in future I must allow Baddeley a feat he has achieved nowhere else, I believe, of firing off in one sentence four superlatives, one of which is in itself a sort of treble hit. Of the whole excursion from Keswick to Buttermere by Borrowdale he says: "This excursion—through the loveliest valley, under the steepest crag, and past three of the most beautiful lakes in the District—is justly accounted the finest drive in Britain."

The picturesque little village of Grange is a suitable point at which to cross the River Derwent and return along the western side of the lake. On the road is Brackenburn, which was Sir Hugh Walpole's home and once housed so many of his remarkable treasures—books, pictures and statues. It was to find additional room for them, particularly for his library, that the extension was built over the garage. It is delightful to wander through Manesty woods which border the lake and so make a leisurely return to Keswick. Hugh Walpole has been so identified with this district that I invoke the reader's tolerance if Wordsworth-like I "here append a few verses of my own on the subject".

HUGH WALPOLE

Hateful the legend as a boy I battened on—
subscription-library hero of the day.
Whilst I was grinding enviously you fattened on
best-seller royalties and easy pay
for rubbish. My unwritten masterpiece was patterned on
no Judas kiss. I wrote the harder way

or not at all: but nothing stopped your writing.
I climbed the hills, I chewed a fruitless cud,
and though I couldn't write I went on fighting
the myth of you and though I was a dud
the more I heard the more I could be biting.
My hatred would have drawn a phantom's blood.

Your profile in the Keswick shops, publicity,
("The home of Judith Paris", said one farm),
"My lakes!" I groaned. I heard of your felicity
in friendship, of your kindness and your charm;
and in my heart I realized the lubricity
of money would make me you. Soul sounded an alarm!

We met among the flesh-pots, London's bait;
A Park-Lane lunch with the new taste of fear.
No chance to assess our subtle love or hate.
Two of a kind inevitably we draw near
but personal relations that day had to wait,
chief guest was the P.M. the Municheer.

The bombs were midwives to what had to be.
Chary in friendship, cold to the printed page
I brought so little, great heart, but I did see
you blazing in the sunset of your age;
Seeing too how well it would have suited me,
I hankered like a bird for a gold cage.

Today in Keswick museum I saw your fame
embalmed in manuscripts superbly bound.
I hate the farms that have erased your name.
I'm glad your library following is sound.
What once I would have changed I wish the same.
But as I watch the leaves fall to the ground—

see time change Manesty woods, I see the night
that will make all things one, where we can't take
the books you wrote or those I didn't write.
Memories may linger for some follower's sake
dust in the sunset whose departing light
Glaramara's crags flash back across the lake.

Borrowdale is the Beethoven of the Lake District valleys.
To some people its appeal is so much greater than that of any
other part that they are content to visit it over and over
again and long to live nowhere else. So was it when I was a
boy. So is it not now, for I have plumped for Applethwaite,
just as it is often later in life that one comes to love Haydn.
The grandeur and beauty of Borrowdale are inexhaustibly
inspiring, but I should imagine that to live there calls for a

certain austerity of spirit. In the upper reaches there are
cottages for which the sun never climbs above the opposite
hill-side from October to March, and even in Grange the
pedestrian who flags will look in vain for an inn or a hired car.

Several of the sights for which Borrowdale is famous are
easily reached from the road along the east side of the lake.
The Falls of Lodore are just behind the hotel. The chasm of
100 feet is magnificent, with wooded cliffs between which the
water may or may not come down in the manner made famous
by Southey. If you happen to go on a dry day you must
either accept the beauty of the scene without water, or con-
sole yourself with the reflection that there is certainly a wet
day coming. A couple of miles farther on, and also close to
the road, is the famous Bowder Stone. Thirty feet high and
60 feet long, estimated to weigh nearly 2,000 tons, it is so
astonishingly poised that two people lying down on opposite
sides of it may shake hands beneath the narrow edge on which
it has come to rest after rolling down the fell-side, whilst the
top, which may be reached by a flight of steps, gives plenty
of room for the visitors to sign the book. A national possession which can be reached by a delightful walk is the
memorial to King Edward VII, formerly Grange Fell and the
Borrowdale Birches, of which 310 acres were purchased in
1910. It looks out on magnificent mountain scenery.

As we approach the famous "Jaws of Borrowdale" there
seems at first no possible exit from the frowning valley head.
In fact, two main branches now divide soon after the
charming little village of Rosthwaite has been passed. The
eastern branch goes left up the valley to Stonethwaite Beck
which itself again divides when Greenup Gill joins Langstrath Beck, which has come tumbling down from Esk Hause
and Angle Tarn. The little hamlet of Stonethwaite stands by
its beck near to Borrowdale's little church. The second main
branch also divides into two at Seatoller, where you may either
take the Sty Head Pass by Seathwaite, the wettest inhabited
place in England with an average annual rainfall of 125 inches
compared with London's average of 23, or you may take the
road over Honister Pass, which thus forms the fourth exit
from the valley head and the only one with a road surface. It
leads to Buttermere.

Up to now we have several times crossed the track of the walk that of all others in the Lake District I have most loved since I first did it a quarter of a century ago. It is the famous Four Passes walk and it would be hard to beat anywhere in the world. In about twenty miles it rings the very heart of the district, and though it makes as strenuous a day as I am ever likely to tackle again it nowhere seriously departs from that concept of walking which does not exclude some puffing and scrambling. It can be done from any of the passes into which it descends but here, since this is how I first did it, let it be from Stonethwaite—and would that it were from the white-washed cottage of the golden-hearted Mrs. Jenkins, who at that time would board you for 7s. 6d. a day and expect two of you to eat a chicken between you by candlelight at the end of the day. Proceed first across the flat head of the valley to Seatoller and there climb Honister Pass till the Crag, which is really part of Fleetwith Pike, yields the viewpoint from which we looked down on the Buttermere valley some time back. If you scorn utterly the motor road which has now successfully covered the dangerous old pass you can from the top of Fleetwith make a descent and join the road when it has got down as near to Buttermere as the farm-house of Gates-garth. You have achieved your first pass and after crossing the green fields at the head of Buttermere begin the fairly sharp ascent of Scarf (or Scarth) Gap. It is marked on the map as a pony track, but there are some rough passages as it makes its way over into Ennerdale between High Crag and Haystacks, with Kirk Fell immediately opposite, Great Gable flanking it on the left, and Pillar on the right, the famous rock an imposing feature. Strange and unforgettable whilst you are still high up is the view of the long, lonely Ennerdale valley, its lake far down and five miles away, the River Liza flowing towards it from your feet. The path descends to the valley bottom and for a short distance pro-ceeds upstream before turning right to climb to the top of Black Sail, the next pass, which leads us over into Mosedale, with its splendid views of the craggy precipices of Scafell, and along Mosedale Beck from which we turned back when tempted to do this walk from Wasdale Head. We can enjoy again this remote spot but need not leave the shelter of Great

Watendlath

Gable, for the Sty Head Pass branches off immediately at Ritson Force and climbs by a long two miles, tiring and stony, till Sty Head Tarn comes into view. It may be that by now Mrs. Jenkins's roast chicken or its equivalent is the most irresistible attraction, in which case you will cross to the Sty Head Beck and descend sharply to Stockley Bridge, with a glance at Tailor Gill on the left, and so return to Seathwaite and Stonethwaite.

On some other occasion you can from the top of Sty Head Pass climb Great Gable. Few mountains equal it either for its own imposing grandeur or the view from the summit. At first sight Aaron Slack, the gully which runs between Green Gable and Great Gable, seems to suggest itself, but it is not recommended. From the highest point on the pass a rough track, marked by cairns, leads in a roundabout but more interesting way to the summit, 2,949 feet. On a boulder near the summit cairn, facing north, is the War Memorial Tablet of the Fell and Rock-climbing Club. It consists of a tablet of bronze engraved on which is a relief map of the neighbouring peaks, those purchased by the Club and presented to the nation through the National Trust being enclosed by a delimiting line. The peaks thus indicated are Kirk Fell, Great Gable, Green Gable, Brandreth, Grey Knotts, Base Brown, Seathwaite Fell, Glaramara, Allen Crags, Great End, Broad Crag and Lingmell.

The Napes Ridges, a little way to the south-west, are famous for the rock-climbing they afford. The mountain-top commands the whole prospect of Wastwater, the green plain beyond, the sea and the Isle of Man. Ennerdale Water is hidden by the Pillar mountain and rock which rise with dramatic abruptness. Scafell Pike and Scafell are also seen at their most impressive. They occupy so much of the foreground as partly to cut off the view to the south, but the main mountains can be seen on three sides, with a strip of the Yorkshire fells far away to the east. The contrast between such exalted mountain pleasures and the delights of the broad, flat valley are part of the characteristic charm of Borrowdale. The wealth of the richly wooded crags that hang over the valley, the rattling stony becks like Langstrath that come gabbling down from the mountains, the remoteness

Great End from the summit of Great Gable ➤

from the world that emphasises the humanity of the little villages—these are perhaps definable elements, though the essence remains elusive. Borrowdale is dramatic and yet lovable, and always unpredictable. I well remember the night in the valley after I first climbed Great Gable. The well of darkness made the stars in the moonless sky shine as I had never seen stars shine before. A rival beam drew me across the meadows and I looked into the lighted interior of one of the farms. Two women were making music. The elder one at the piano had a cowl of white hair, like Irene Forsyte in that glimpse we get of her in old age. The younger woman, who was singing, held up a candle to light the page. The music that floated out mingled with the sound of water that filled the valley. The solitary candle indoors, the great blazing stars in the sky, the smell of unseen garden flowers, the mountain air. . . . Ah, Borrowdale remembered!

CHAPTER XI

Thirlmere, Helvellyn and Ullswater

IT is tempting to return to Keswick from the head of Borrowdale by taking the pony track from Rosthwaite up to Watendlath and thus by an easy walk through fell and woods to the famous viewpoint at Ashness Bridge, enjoying in reverse the scenery described in the last chapter. But we must cover new ground. A path from Watendlath climbs over the side of Armboth Fell and drops immediately to Thirlmere, whilst another passes close to Blea Tarn, dropping by Harrop Tarn to the lower end of the lake opposite Wythburn. But all this block of elevated moorland I have always found sodden underfoot and hard going. The reward by either of the paths I have mentioned comes when you reach the brink of the fell and see below you the whole length of Thirlmere lying immediately under Helvellyn. This rises with a preponderating impression of mass, undistinguished by notable peaks or crags, but a mighty mountain. We are looking at its long and less exciting side, but as I have a mind to take us on the walk along its ridge and to start it properly from the southern end we will not descend to Thirlmere, and indeed the best that it has to offer is seen from where we are.

Writers who could remember what had to go sixty-odd years ago when Thirlmere became a source of water supply for Manchester record with sorrow its vanished charms. All this district was rich in legends of a good strong old-fashioned flavour—a nocturnal marriage and a murdered bride, strange lights in windows, and uncanny figures at Armboth's haunted farm; a black dog that swam the lake "o' nights"; a murder which the country folk, as usual, commemorated by planting

a cutting from the ancient Yggdrasil, the mythological
Scandinavian tree whose branches and roots sustain the
world—all waiting for Sir Hall Caine to work into his novel
The Shadow of a Crime. Personally, I find more interesting
the fact that Miss Jackson, whose family occupied Armboth
Farm for many generations, married a Russian, Count
Ossalinsky. When Manchester wanted the land they made a
generous offer, but she asked for three times as much, went
to law and won. The Countess Ossalinsky died in 1902 aged
eighty-one. Wythburn near the foot of Thirlmere on the
east side had also a long history. Here manorial courts were
held and a local parliament wrote by-laws, mostly on agricultural matters, called "The Pains and Penalties of Wythburn". Today there is scarcely anything here but the church
with its uneven floor and tiny chancel.

To leave Stonethwaite in this way is to miss much interesting scenery. Let us rather follow Stonethwaite Beck for a
mile and pause at the footbridge to consider alternative ways.
Greenup Gill comes down from the left and you can follow its
course, guiding yourself by a prominent rock called Lining
Crag to Greenup Edge from where it is easy to descend the
Wythburn valley on your left or proceed straight on down
Far Easedale Gill and so comfortably to Grasmere. Alternatively, at the Stonethwaite footbridge you may choose Langstrath and follow the beck which joins that of Greenup to
meet Stonethwaite Beck at this point. You enter this desolate but fascinating valley between the guardian crags Eagle
and Bull and climb under the rugged slopes of Glaramara
amid scenery which as the woods drop behind seems to be
compounded entirely of stone and water—interesting, unpredictable volcanic stone, and water that is everywhere clear,
sometimes rushing and musical, sometimes welling into silent
pools. Presently you come to the foot of Stake Pass zig-
zagging unmistakably up a steep slope with a tributary beck
on the left. If you choose instead to pursue Langstrath Beck
to its source you are well placed to climb the Scafell group.
If you follow the pass to its head you can explore the Langdale Pikes. As we shall do this from Ambleside, the best
capture from here would be Bow Fell, the wonderful outline
of which has been the principal feature throughout the

length of Langstrath. We see here the opposite side to that which looks down Eskdale. They present an identical outline, unlike the Langdale Pikes, which one always feels rather cheated about on discovering that the familiar outline, so impressive from the south and east, is the only eminence they have. To the north and west they simply stretch away in moorlands of equal height, and to what you might call an all-round giant like Bow Fell, they are negligible protuberances. They are not, of course, to blame if the mind's eye erroneously constructs for them other sides to match their famous façade. All the same it is very satisfactory of Bow Fell to be the same, and that same so fine and imposing, on all sides.

The long, high mass into which the Langdale Pikes merge to the north is strangely featureless, but its elevated top provides an unrivalled platform for the whole of this central part of the mountains. To the south-east the crags of Pavey Ark drop sheer into Stickle Tarn, another familiar feature of the view from Windermere, but stretching north Thunacar Knott, Sergeant Man, High Raise and High White Stones provide the platform I have mentioned, for all of which High Raise seems the ideal name. We noticed on the summit of Great Gable how the dramatic upward spring of Pillar and the impressive crags of Scafell Pike cut off sections of the view. This upland enjoys the advantage of being featureless in itself and its immediate vicinity and has an uninterrupted circular view—Coniston Old Man, Bow Fell, Scafell Pikes, Pillar, Gable, Buttermere Fells, Skiddaw, Saddleback, the Helvellyn ridge, the Rydal fells, the full length of Windermere.

By whichever of these routes you choose let me invite you to get yourself to the main road nearly half-way between Grasmere and Dunmail Raise, opposite Helm Crag, that we may begin the ascent of Helvellyn, that most enjoyable expedition whereby we shall return to Keswick in circumstances as different as well could be from those in which the motorists, the cyclists and the coaches stream in the same direction along the eastern road of poor old Thirlmere. If we were going by road the western bank has all the advantages.

Helvellyn is a classic mountain in the sense which permits that adjective for a work of acknowledged excellence. It is indeed one of the *unbegreiflich hohen Werke*, glorious as on the day of creation were it not for the litter-fiends. It seems to me to have everything a mountain can offer: by our standards, mighty mass (it rises to 3,118 feet, our highest after the Scafells), interest, beauty and fame. It naturally is not conquered without reasonable exertion, but it is not inaccessible by routes which, unlike Baddeley, I do not find tedious, to a summit which, I agree with Symonds, gives on the right day the best of all the views from the bigger fells. Its culmination is intensely dramatic. When I look at photographs of Swirrel Edge and Striding Edge and think that I have ventured along them I am recurrently astonished at my prowess, and it matters nothing to me that that achievement provokes in others only an indulgent smile. It is characteristic of Helvellyn to grant me a hazardous and inspiring physical experience such as my own resources could never reasonably expect to achieve. Flattering the mountain-tops we have heard of; I like a mountain whose top returns the compliment. If a man is known by his favourites I am com-complacent in my choice of mountains. As for those who leave litter in the shelter—they should be prohibited from approaching nearer than Salford. It would be as difficult to persuade me that Helvellyn is not a creditable favourite as that The Twilight of the Gods is just a trick of the light.

There are four routes by which Helvellyn is normally climbed. From Thirlspot or Wythburn everything is sacrificed to the shortness of the approach. The two that are interesting all the way are from Patterdale or from Grasmere, climbing as we now propose to by Grisedale Pass. Soon after you leave the main road you see Tongue Gill coming down on the right of the tongue itself which blocks the valley. Our path is the one to the left along the slope of Seat Sandal to Grisedale Tarn, one of the most fascinating of all the tarns that are such an interesting feature of the Lake District. Although it is at a height of 1,768 feet it lies deep-set among the bare slopes of Fairfield, Seat Sandal and Dollywaggon Pike, across which you can clearly see the track ahead zig-zagging to the highest ridge of Helvellyn between which and Seat Sandal appears the range of fells from Derwentwater to Crummock with Grisedale Pike. This is no kinsman of the tarn at our feet, but neighbour of that Causey Pike, also visible, which, with Grasmoor, forms the last major group of mountains in the north-west of the Lake District, and which we have already encountered rising between Crummock and the Whinlatter Pass upwards of twelve miles away as we look straight across from our present position. The water of the tarn, quite free from rushes and weeds, and surrounded not by precipices but by slopes of rough grass, is beautifully clear.

It is possible in about half an hour from this point to reach the top of Fairfield and the temptation is difficult to resist, for half an hour is little enough. Moreover the brief interval may be delightfully filled by evoking the recollection of a tremendous ascent about a century ago, of which there has been preserved for us a fabulous account. It is a period piece between which and our own day the rock climbers at Wasdale Head fifty years ago occupy a nicely balancing midway position. We noted there how comparatively recent was the rise of the British mountaineer, and that his predecessor up to then had been the strenuous walker. In the volume *Recollections of the Cambridge Union* to which the editor, Mr. Percy Cradock, contributed such a graceful and perspicacious account of the nineteenth century, there is a characteristically evocative background to the incident on Fairfield on which I cannot help but enlarge as we lose our breath during this brief ascent, or sit regaining it on top. It was still the celibate world of an unreformed Cambridge, but it was a world that was drawing to a close. The Evangelical discipline had abated the excesses of the preceding generations, both manners and scholarship were greatly improved, and as Mr. Cradock says,

Undergraduates' interest concentrated very much on the Tripos, which aroused the kind of enthusiasm nowadays kept for games. There was some sport, though of an unorganized sort, rowing and cricket. There was riding for those who could afford it. But the great exercise, expressing the frugal and strenuous spirit of the age, was walking. A sound walker was expected to do fifteen miles in three hours, without special training or being the worse for it the next day, and probably there is no more characteristic figure from the Cambridge of

this time than the Reading-Man setting out with his companion in the early afternoon on the Grantchester Grind,
sober-suited, in Berlin wool gloves, and the tails of his frock-
coat flapping in the wind.

It was a period of great peace of which the outlook was
focused in the Union.

In December of that year there was a motion of the Society,
passed with one opposing vote:

That the political and social history of England since the
peace of 1815 has been one of real and great social improve-
ment, and there is reason to trust—unless by the wilful
fault of the present generation—the future will be still happier
than the past.

This is the Union of 1851—its members solemnly surveying
the course of history to date, and looking forward, after all
not unreasonably, to a future even more contented. It is a
pleasant picture, and one which seems to us now very remote.
Our only wonder is what kind of foreboding there rose in the
mind of the one dissentient.

The figure I am stalking, perhaps with something of the
discursiveness of that more leisurely age is James Payn,
of Trinity College, later novelist, contributor to Dickens's
various magazines and subsequently editor of *Chambers's
Journal* and the *Cornhill Magazine*. In 1852 he was President
of the Union and since the present book is dedicated to one
of his successors in that office, and written by another, and
since all have had in common a love both of that society
and of the Lake District I hope this gathering and colloquy
on the mountain-top of Fairfield will be indulged as of
fortuitous interest; with no improper hint of apostolic
succession.

With three companions James Payn set out from Ambleside.

These were the chief of the necessaries which my sagacity
procured for our night-bivouac and tremendous ascent: thirty-
six bottles of bitter beer, two bottles of gin, two bottles of
sherry, one gallon of water; four loaves of bread, one leg of
lamb, one leg of mutton, two fowls, one tongue, half-pound of
cigars, four carriage-lamps, and two packs of playing-cards.
We had also a large tent, which was carried upon the back of
a horse. Three men were necessary to pitch this tabernacle

and to carry the provisions. About five o'clock in the afternoon we started for the mountains with a huge train of admirers, forming the largest cavalcade that had ever left Ambleside before. But most of our camp-followers quitted us at the foot of Nab Scar, at Rydal, where the tremendous ascent was to begin. . . . At last we reached the top of the humps or aiguilles of Fairfield, a little beyond which we had determined to fix our tent. Here we caught the sound of a fowling-piece, fired off at Ambleside, no doubt in exultation at our success; and X acknowledged the compliment by tying his pocket-handker-chief on to his umbrella, and waving it three times.

We can look out and share their enjoyment of the view, though we are unlikely to settle down as they did to a game of cards inside the tent. Payn gives a description of the peacefulness which reigned for a long time within the tent until there were heard the undertones of a rising wind. Suddenly the gale burst out in full fury. . . .

In an instant, an unknown force hurled me from my kneeling posture, prostrate upon the ground, and some monster at the same moment seemed to leap upon me with inconceivable violence. The whole party experienced a sensation precisely similar. The last stormpuff had carried our tent clean off its pegs.

For some minutes we were inextricably involved amidst guides, bottles, friends, cards, carriage lamps and cold meats, besides finding a difficulty in breathing. I struggled as violently as any . . . and was the first to find myself ankle deep in the coldest water . . . The whole concern had rolled somehow into a morass, and it was a matter of great good fortune it did so, instead of rolling into the fire which had been kindled immediately above it. . . .

(Then they all wriggled about like eels extricating them-selves. . . . It was one o'clock in the morning. They began blaming one another for having undertaken this mad trip. . . . Time dragged on. . . .)

Then, in the cold grey morning, a mist came over Fairfield, which presently resolved itself into a drizzle, then into rain. More limp, discreditable persons than the climbers could scarcely be imagined as they came down into the valley. We did not thoroughly appreciate our miserable condition until somebody at Rydal offered to lend us *umbrellas*. He might as well have offered mackintoshes to a family of otters!

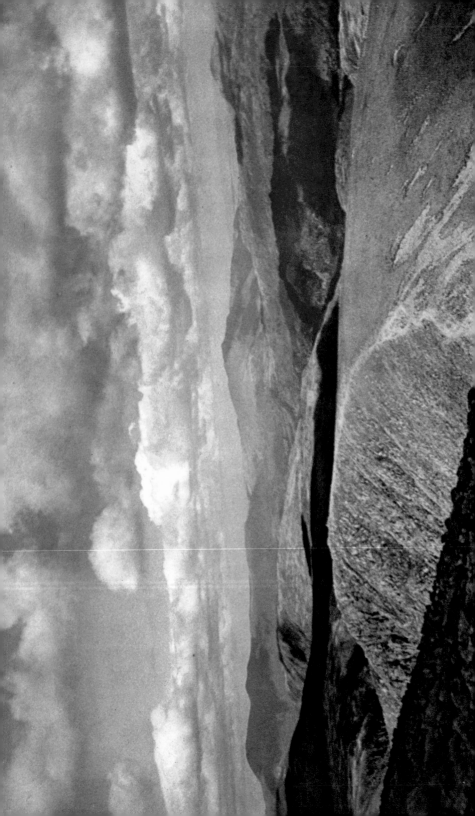

Did Mr. Cradock say that walking "expressed the frugal
and strenuous spirit of the age"? Anyhow let us display
some of these qualities ourselves and with no further misleading dallying with the idea of tabernacles on mountains,
get ourselves over Dollywaggon Pike, by that path so clearly
indicated, to the crest of Helvellyn. Down below at the head
of Thirlmere is the little mountain, just over 1,000 feet, of
Great Howe, which Rossetti, at his own suggestion and to
the astonishment of his host Hall Caine, who lived nearby
at the entrance to the Vale of St. John, climbed, after having
consumed on the way from London a quantity of chloral
that would have been sufficient to destroy the entire Hall
Caine household. "He awoke fresh and in good spirits towards the middle of the afternoon and breakfasted heartily."
From the top of the hill the view was such that Rossetti was
much impressed: "I'm not one of those who care about
scenery, but this is marvellous and the colour is wonderful",
he said. His spirits were high, and when, on beginning the
descent, he lost his footing and slithered some distance
through the bracken before Hall Caine could stop him, he
only laughed and said:

"Don't be afraid, I always go up on my feet and come
down on a broader basis."

Now they are what I would call exotics in the Lake District.

From the summit of Helvellyn the view is dominated by
mountains. It is indeed, as Wordsworth said

> A record of commotion
> Which a thousand ridges yield.

Not a valley can be seen, a fact as unexpected as that not a
gleam of water in the canals of Venice can be seen from the
top of the campanile on the Piazza in the centre of the city.
On the other hand, Helvellyn's height and central position
allow every important mountain in the Lake District to be
seen as well as a wide stretch of Morecambe Bay, part of the
Cumbrian coast, the Solway Firth and the mountains of
Dumfries-shire. The lakes immediately visible are Windermere, Esthwaite, Coniston and Ullswater, and by walking
forward a few hundred yards one may add Thirlmere and
Bassenthwaite to make six.

E.L.—14

Green Gable from the summit of Great Gable

Helvellyn throws out great spurs to the east, the two most notable being those which enfold Red Tarn, Striding Edge and Swirrel Edge. The eminence at the end of the latter is Catchedicam. This eye and tongue troubler is a less corrupt version of a good old name in its alternative form Catstycam. The wild cat left a name here as on Catbells, sty as in Sty Head is a path, and cam is a ridge as in Cam Spout. Cam, like the majority of Cumbrian names, is Norse. Helvellyn is one of the rare Celtic names.

The terrier who for three months guarded the remains of the poet Charles Gough, who fell from Striding Edge in 1805 is famous. She was unable to find food enough to preserve the family to which she gave birth but ranged far and wide for bits of carrion sheep to maintain life on her long vigil. Both Wordsworth and Scott commemorated the little yellow rough-haired creature. The former immediately recognized as the most beautiful of Scott's lines those that can still get through one's defences with a poignant thrust.

How long didst thou think that his silence was slumber?
When the wind waved his garment how oft did'st thou start?

Little Foxie is outstanding even among the many dogs who play a great part in the annals of the Lake District just as they do in its day-to-day life. From the very path down to Patterdale below us and in many other lonely places I have seen the solitary hound, head down, trekking back mile after mile over the mountain pass to a distant home. Similarly the average shepherd's dog from time to time achieves some wonderful rescues of Herdwick sheep which have strayed on to dangerous jutting crags, for though Herdwicks can go anywhere they can't always get back. It is a familiar feature of dog shows that owners seem to take on the characteristics of their favourite breed. Here the dog often seems to reverse the complimentary process and accept from the farmer a philosophic attitude of indulgent but firm, persistently firm, and patient benevolence towards the cussedness of his grey-woolled charges whose venturesomeness may require an hour's coaxing along rock ledges or a day spent in fetching ropes and help.

Instead of making any of the four usual descents let us

Borrowdale from Taylor Force ◂

take advantage of the fact that a track runs north over the entire chain of Helvellyn which stretches over seven miles from Grisedale Tarn nearly to Threlkeld and comprises seven summits over 2,700 feet high. Of these, reckoning from south to north, Dollywaggon Pike is the first, and Helvellyn and the Low Man the second and third. The others in order are Whiteside, Raise, Stybarrow Dodd and Great Dodd. From the top of Great Dodd there is a beautiful view over Keswick and its vale, and we may either get to it by dropping down the side of Clough Head to Birkett Bank in the fertile Vale of St. John or strike right ahead over White Pike and down to Threlkeld. In the meantime we can sit on the green rounded dome of Great Dodd and ponder for a few moments about Lakeland industries of which we are reminded by the sight of the quarries down below at Threlkeld. This is the source of the grey granite that paves the Cumberland roads, and roads farther afield, and in the past few years it has been poured by thousands of tons into the concrete which has made the atomic piles of Sellafield, a constant stream of grey-white chips from the quarries which cut into the sides of the mountains near Keswick. Lorries by the hundred still carry it to the new atomic power station at Calder Hall. The newest of industries is greatly dependent upon one of the oldest industries in the world.

The Cumberland mountains have such a variety of rock formations that it is natural that quarrying should have achieved importance among local industries. Most famous of all Lakeland rocks is the "Buttermere Green" slate from the quarries on Honister Pass. The Honister quarries have scarred the neighbouring mountain-sides but in doing so have provided a stone which is the delight of those people who like all houses and other buildings to harmonize with the countryside, for a roof or wall of Buttermere slate will melt into the landscape almost as soon as it is built. The top of Honister where this slate is quarried and split is what script-writers used to call a man's world and the men who live and work there are among the toughest of men, and always have been. Tales have been told of the life there in the old days that sound like stories of pioneer towns in the West of America, when the quarrymen sought their pleasure

in long-spaced trips into Borrowdale and Keswick, but today
the quarryman, still tough, has his home in the dale, and
some take "busmen's" holidays rock-climbing. Part of their
old quarters is now a youth hostel.

There is gold in the Cumberland mountains, but it is no
longer an economic proposition to work it. Queen Elizabeth I
is reported to have said that her gold mines in Cumberland
were of more value than the rest of England. Today Gold-
scope in Newlands is but a name. But there was a black
gold which attracted an influx of German miners to the
Keswick district—plumbago, the stuff of which pencils are
made. The Germans left some descendants and some names,
but the pipes of plumbago were worked out and it is no longer
mined. The town of Keswick has still a pencil-making
industry of world-wide fame. Little industries were sited
where water power was available and remain, though the
electric motor has replaced the mill-wheel. There is a large
factory given to making wooden bobbins for the textile trade
on the banks of the River Greta above Keswick, and here
and there in the dales there are men turning native timbers
into bowls, cake stands and candlesticks.

Industries of the past have left their scars on the face of
Lakeland, but time has been kind and Nature has laid a
swathe of green over the smaller spoil heaps, and the weather
has converted the smears of larger piles of new-hewn rock
to blend with the screes on the mountain-sides.

But it is not to expatiate rather inordinately on the
industries of the district that I have brought us thus far
back north so much as to ensure that the proper approach is
made to Ullswater. Those who have run through their time,
as I have through my space, without allowing enough to do
justice to this most beautiful lake cannot afford the dis-
appointment that awaits those who come first over the
Kirkstone Pass by road or more energetically by the Sticks
Pass over the tops between Stybarrow Dodd and Raise. The
approach from Penrith to Pooley Bridge, followed by a sail
up the lake is first-rate. Then the lake is first seen from its
foot, in this case the north, as it should be. But there is an
unrivalled approach from the road at which we have just

been looking which runs from Keswick to Penrith. You turn off near Troutbeck station (nothing to do with the Windermere Troutbeck) traverse a few commonplace miles, and arrive at Dockray, a well-placed hamlet about half a mile beyond Matterdale church, restored but interesting. From here the descent for just over a mile by a steep but well-made road to the side of the lake is one long process of beauty revealing itself stage by stage.

Ullswater is of the long river-lake pattern and makes two sharp bends. As a result, it is divided into three distinct reaches, but there is nothing geometric about their proportions and characteristics. Near to Dockray are Aira Force and nearer the water's edge Lyulph's Tower, an eighteenth-century shooting-box standing possibly on the site of one built by Lyulph, first baron of Greystoke. The name is said to be in origin of Ulf or l'ulf, whence Ullswater. The beauty of this walk resides particularly in the way the finest stretch of the lake comes gradually into view between Gowbarrow Park on the left and Glencoyne on the right. The lower stretch of Ullswater is comparatively tame. After the middle stretch which now confronts us with Long Crag and Slee Fell, the "Dodds" of Place Fell across the water, the upper reach carries the scenery to its most beautiful. It is an indication of how sharp is the bend in the lake that Patterdale is hidden from us by Birk Fell, with Place Fell behind it, and the promontory of Silver Hill all on the other side of the lake which bends right round them. From Patterdale to Pooley Bridge there is a good road along the north side of the lake and a rougher one on the other side from Pooley Bridge to How Town.

Patterdale establishes a great hold on the affections of those who visit it. It is a delightful place for a holiday, and more than anywhere else I know the village and this part of the valley are a microcosm in which you feel you could live and at the end have known something of most aspects of life—certainly as much as a man might absorb without troubling the great world outside. The devoted village priest, the doctor, the philosopher with his market garden, the hard-working women in the families which provide such excellent accommodation, the great house, now put at the disposal of

the Y.M.C.A., the church, the pub, the tillers of the few
green fields, the occupants of the fine stone houses and the
charming cottages—there is everything here from the silence
of the lake and the lonely places among the hills to the busy
humanity of the village. It was characteristically percipient
of the *Manchester Guardian* in a recent General Election,
seeking somewhere that would reflect all sections of the
community, to go to Patterdale. All things that divide men
elsewhere divide them here, but to a degree not possible
everywhere this community can also be united—the day the
steamer was overwhelmed and sank, the day of grief when
the local mining operations took their last toll, these and
many other things make up the life of a very real community
to which it is a privilege to be admitted as a grateful visitor.

Along the main road lies the hamlet of Glenridding. Then
comes Stybarrow Crag. Interesting valleys run off to the
left down which come the becks which rise on the Helvellyn
range. The first and most important is Grisedale, where from
Patterdale itself one may make the ascent of Helvellyn or
turn aside at Grisedale Tarn along the track by which we
approached from near Grasmere. Glenridding and Glencoyne
each have their dale. Then comes the road from Dockray
by which we arrived, Lyulph's Tower and Gowbarrow Park
where Wordsworth saw the host of golden daffodils. The
charm of the walk to Pooley Bridge is not so much in the
places of interest on the road as in the changing vistas of
the lake opening so easily before one, sometimes between
tree trunks or picturesque rocks, under crags on the opposite
shore, or open sweeps of moorland fringed with green pasture.
At Pooley Bridge the River Eamont leaves the lake and in
the gardens that run down from the back of the houses to
the river they have, for as long as men much older than I
am can remember, always planted their new potatoes on
Good Friday. The Sun is an inn of which many generations
of fishermen and others have happy recollections. It is one
of the farewell points of the Lake District proper which I
have mentioned elsewhere, and the impulse to turn back and
return to Patterdale along the other side of the lake is almost
irresistible. In his *Guide to the Lakes* Wordsworth includes
an account of a visit to Ullswater which is a first-class

example of his luminous powers of observation and expression. I can only refer the reader to his account. His visit was paid in November, and if I draw here on my own notes of a walk along the bank to How Town it is in no misguided spirit of emulation, but for the possible interest of some contrasts, since I was there for an early, sunny Easter.

It was one of those March days that are like a quotation from summer. In the hot sun the sight of the snow on the mountain-tops was thrilling and seemed to send down cool air for us as we walked. A heron rose. A flock of brilliant white gulls, startling against the brown earth, followed a tractor-plough. Horses, birds, lambs and bullocks, all were in spring mood. The lake, as we walked along, was a great mirror, reflecting the hill-side opposite, the frieze of sheep and the white houses built by the English who had made their homes there. In its brilliance it did not seem sometimes to be an English scene.

The larches, the catkins, wood chopped and lying. Stone. The mountains marched with us. We came to a gate-house where they were burning heaps of leaves. The bird-cherry was out, white against the deepening blue sky, loud with bees.

By Sharrow Bay a tiny stream ran into the lake. We sat by the miniature estuary and ate some of our sandwiches. For a time everything seemed white—houses, sheep, white lambs, white violets—there was even a white doe among the fallow deer. Then on the opposite side the little red Post Office van ran upside down in the water the length of the lake. Rooks taxied in the fields.

We walked on and the road became rougher. The last gardens with their yellow forsythia were left behind. The last building was a simple hostelry. We sat there and drank beer and listened to the curlews calling and the ceaseless singing of the chaffinches. Smells of smoke and earth and farms. Pink tips on the tail-feathers of partridges. Buzzards sailing round and round on motionless wings. Little becks purling down the hill-side behind and across the last meadow into the lake. In front of us was a brown ploughed field with an orange-coloured farm set in it like a child's painting.

When we left the inn the road became a track, climbing now, so that when we looked back the lake, limpid, with all

Stonethwaite, Borrowdale

its reflections, was dropping below us. The track was sometimes stony, sometimes grassy, smelling exotically of thyme.
As the lake released us with a last just-audible lapping, rough
rocky slopes towering above, covered with junipers, received
us. On. Upwards. It was easy. Upwards to the blue, blue sky.

Amazingly we came to a tiny church, rough, simple, hewn
out of the stone of the hill-side. Windows of clear glass
framed pictures of the mountains outside. I read the notices
about when the services were held and where the snow-plough
was kept, for when needed. Through the church door we
could see the rocky little churchyard. A thrush on a yew-
tree suddenly burst into loud, cheerful song, full-toned,
repetitive, a wonderful solo performance.

The old Martindale church has an interesting interior.
The new Martindale church is at Cowgarth. You pass it if
you return to Patterdale by Rampsgill, climbing the hause
between Hallin Fell and Steel Knotts and taking care to
leave the long valley of Rampsgill on the left, and follow
Boardale to the head of Boardale Hause, 1,260 feet, at which
point there is a sudden and wonderful view of the surrounding
valleys, fells and lakes. Some of these valleys are among the
most remote in the district. The whole area is most attractive
to the walker who prefers to let his luggage stay put for the
length of his holiday whilst he explores. He may thus ascend
Place Fell, visit Angle Tarn with its attractively indented
shore, and also do more justice than we were able to earlier
to Haweswater and the High Street range.

We must leave Patterdale, travelling first through well-
cultivated pastoral country, succeeded by wooded crags.
The road skirts the square sheet of Brothers Water and
climbs steadily to the summit of Kirkstone Pass. The inn has
an exhilarating top-of-the-world feeling. Often there is an
unexpected flurry of snow in the air of what elsewhere is a
summer day. Far below, in the distance, you can see where
Barrow thrusts into the sea. Here we let the Windermere
road diverge more attractively to the left, for it will take us
down Troutbeck whose lower reaches we have already
explored. We will risk our necks on the rough, steep road
that descends to Ambleside, 1,300 feet below in three bone-
shaking miles.

Langdale Blea Tarn, looking north-east ➤

CHAPTER XII

Ambleside, Grasmere and Rydal

F ROM Troutbeck Bridge on our left which we visited
from Windermere to the point at which we began the
ascent of Helvellyn, the road in about eight or nine
miles runs through Ambleside, Rydal and Grasmere—along
the green and famous valley of the River Rothay which
collects its tributaries and becomes recognizably the Rothay
near where we looked up Tongue Gill. It flows through both
Grasmere and Rydal and enters Windermere in the little
estuary of the River Brathay which has flowed under
Skelwith Bridge from Elter Water. Beyond there the
Brathay would lead us back up to Little Langdale, the
Three-Shires-Stone at Wrynose and the origins of the River
Duddon. The valley of Great Langdale waves us back to the
mountains and the central massif. These two Langdale
valleys and that of the Rothay, roughly the green country
that lies around Loughrigg Fell, constitute our last section
in this sketchy account of the Lake District. We may perhaps be said to have reached the heart of the matter. Everywhere is sacred ground. If, coming last to it I have less
space than it might claim, that is not entirely unintentional
for this is the most written-about part and the best known.
I could have devoted a book as long as this to this one area.
Many others in fact have done so, and they must reconcile
us to touching briefly on much that should be lingered over.

We sometimes say of a friend that his faults are on the
surface; so it is with those of Ambleside. They are obvious
but easily overlooked or avoided. They arise, mostly in the
main street, from the advantages Ambleside enjoys as a
centre for a large portion of the Lake District. But if there

is sometimes an impression of a thoroughfare roaring with traffic that crushes the hikers back on to the crowded pavements and into the picture-postcard shops, sucking ice-cream with absorption or signalling loudly to each other, it is easy to escape. The little town is surrounded by mountain grandeur, but it is set in a broad, park-like plain. Delightful walks are immediately accessible without climbing, and yet many of the mountains are visited as conveniently from here as anywhere. Our friend James Payn described it as "the axle at the wheel of beauty". The town has many enviably situated houses and picturesque corners. I venture to disagree with the view that the spire of Sir Gilbert Scott's church is a mistake, even though it is a view that the architect is said to share. One does not automatically respond to an architect's invitation to admire nor need we condemn as instructed. To my mind the spire here, as in many places surrounded by hills, breaks the skyline in an interesting way from many points of view. And at night, watching from the window the moonlight on the roofs I have heard St. Mary's spill its beautiful chimes on the air and thought the spire gave the little town just an air of—I was going to say somewhere foreign—but I think it is perhaps just a change of key in the ever-changing English scene.

On the Saturday in the Octave of Saint Anne the church is the scene of the famous rush-bearing ceremony when a procession of children is formed carrying crosses and designs made of rushes and flowers. A similar ceremony is observed at Grasmere on the Saturday within the Octave of the patronal saint, Oswald, who is honoured on October 5th. Musgrave, Warcop and Urswick-in-Furness also have rush-bearings. The ceremony, once a common one in London churches, dates from the days before carpets replaced rushes as floor-coverings. Quite near the centre of the town a tiny hump-backed bridge over Stock Beck carries a proportionately small two-storey building. A stone staircase links the two rooms outside. Goblin work you think, but, in fact, three hundred years ago it was the summerhouse of Ambleside Hall and was surrounded by apple trees. It is now, appropriately, a curiosity shop, the property safeguarded by the National Trust, which also owns the Borrans Roman camp near Waterhead. The walks and excursions from Ambleside are famous and well sign-posted. Stock Gill Force, Wansfell Pike, Jenkin Crag, Scandale, Loughrigg, Clappersgate, and others—they should none of them be missed. The literary atmosphere thickens at every step. We have perhaps had enough culture in this book to make some people feel for their guns, but they should keep away from the Lake District. We will take at least one walk, even if it has to be heel and toe and even eyes right and eyes left, that strings together many of the interesting associations. For those with leisure enough there is so much to learn. You may, for instance, have the feeling of actually sharing the working of a poet's mind as you read Keats's description in a letter of Stock Gill Fall or stand with Wordsworth by Loughrigg Tarn in the splendour of a July noon and watch his gaze drop from the Langdale Pikes, soaring above, to the grass at his feet where the shadow of a daisy was thrown on a smooth stone. The tiny phenomenon was seminal enough to produce one of Wordsworth's last poems beginning:

> So fair, so sweet, withal so sensitive,
> Would that the little flowers were born to live
> Conscious of half the pleasure that they give,
>
> That to this mountain-daisy's self was known
> The beauty of its star-shaped shadow thrown
> On the smooth surface of this naked stone!

One of the pleasures of reading about eighteenth-century London is to find the same figures crossing and re-crossing the scene. Nearly all the people of note knew each other, and so it is in this rural scene, particularly of the early first half of the last century. Here is Charles Lloyd, the friend of Lamb, living by the Brathay. He suffered a mental breakdown and was removed to an asylum. He escaped back to de Quincey's cottage and poured out his tragic confidences so that years afterwards de Quincey could hear on quiet nights the sound of the Brathay in its rocky bed as "choral chanting—distant, solemn, saintly". And here is Lloyd's sister Agatha (whose great-great-grandson was Laurence Binyon) trying in a letter to describe the mind of Coleridge, who had been staying with her. On one day Southey joined them for an hour and whilst he was there Wordsworth called. Of the various conjunctions of these stars that occurred at various times, my own favourite is ironically enough not in the Lake District but is a triumph for the London faction. This was at Haydon's rooms in Covent Garden in 1817, "the glorious party" at which Haydon entertained Wordsworth, Lamb, Keats, Ritchie, Monkhouse and, inadvertently, the comptroller of stamps, who provoked Lamb to such uproarious ribaldry. One seems to hear the living accent in Wordsworth's reiterated protest: "Charles! my dear Charles!" just as one delightedly does in the very first reported remark of the evening: "Now," said Lamb to Wordsworth, "you old Lake poet, you rascally poet, why do you call Voltaire dull?"

We must leave this indefensible digression and take the path that passes St. Mary's Church and leads towards the Rothay to Pelter Bridge, where you may turn away from the main road and climb Loughrigg Terrace either to descend to Rydal or to make the extended circuit of Rydal Water and Grasmere. Among the notable houses you could see (leaving Dove Cottage and Rydal Mount aside) is right at the outset, the Knoll, the home of Harriet Martineau which had so many famous visitors. Among the many books written there surely one of the most remarkable was her translation and summary of the works of the philosopher Comte, of which he himself thought so highly that he recommended it to his pupils in preference to his own original work. The road goes past Fox How, which Arnold of Rugby built in 1823 (Wordsworth designed the chimneys). Nearby, Fox Gill was the home of W. E. Forster, Irish Secretary and educational reformer.

At Loughrigg Holme lived Dora, Wordsworth's daughter, as Mrs. Quillinan, and at the house just opposite the Stepping Stones, by which Dorothy Wordsworth was painted, lived Wordsworth's last surviving grandson, Gordon Wordsworth, who died in 1935. More notable houses await us on the Rydal road beyond the Knoll, but their owners, associations, visitors and histories are too numerous to detail.

Moreover, before we settle down to pottering, we have one more major expedition to enjoy—the Langdales and Scafell.

Shorter walks will soon fill in what we have not seen of
Little Langdale, for we have looked across this delightful
green valley from Hawkshead, from Oxenfell, which divides
it from Coniston, and from the Three-Shires-Stone on
Wrynose Pass. The best way to approach Great Langdale is
by taking the Wrynose road till, just past Little Langdale
Tarn, on the open fell, a much inferior road turns sharply
to the right and climbs straight up the side of Lingmoor Fell
past Blea Tarn, getting steeper all the way. There is, however, an early reward, and many later ones. Hardly have
you begun to climb before there arises over the hollow in
front something like the tip of the finger of God. This is
Pike o' Stickle, isolated for a minute or two, then joined by
its companion Harrison Stickle. The dramatic way in which
they thus present themselves is one of the surprises of the
district, and as they draw to their full height, Loft Crag and
Gimmer Crag hanging precipitously between them, it is
difficult to believe that mountain face is only a comparatively
modest 2,400 feet, or that one had any sense of disappoint-
ment on seeing them from behind. The difference is the
same as between looking at the gable end of a house from the
pavement and looking at it from the chimneys of the next
house in the row.

Blea Tarn is now on the left, a recurring challenge to the
photographer, whose camera has many advantages over the
human eye in the matter of perspective. Bow Fell, Crinkle
Crags and Pike o' Blisco come into view, and beyond the
top of the pass but still about 700 feet above sea-level is the
gateway to what is now a farm but was described by Wordsworth as the cottage of the Solitary, the "one bare dwelling,
one above, no more". The guide books refer one respectfully
to *The Excursion, Book Two*. The spirit of irony, however,
is mischievous with Wordsworth in these parts. Below the
ridge that separates the two Langdales at a cottage called
Hackett lived Jonathan and Betty Yewdale. Mr. G. S.
Sandilands has, without comment, printed in his *Lakeland
Anthology* three fragments. The first is a note by Wordsworth in prose saying that when his children had whooping
cough they stayed with the Yewdales for a change of air,
and the Wordsworths took tea with them on fine summer

afternoons "so that we became intimately acquainted with the characters, habits and lives of these good, and, let me say, in the main wise people". In the second extract they appear in *The Excursion*, a perfect Hermann and Dorothea bathed in the transforming light of the poet's imagination, whilst the matron explains with what toil they gain the bread for which they pray "and for the wants provide, of sickness, accident and helpless age". In the third Doric prose extract, another contemporary writer, A. C. Gibson describes how Jonathan had attended a funeral at Coniston and failed to return till a neighbour saw Betty bringing him home. "Fund him? Ey, I fund him . . ." at the Black Dog with a lot more whom she laid into, sent the beef steaks and the frying pan flying, dragged her Jonathan out but was so ashamed to be seen on the road with him she made him creep into a sheep hole in the wall, "an' when I gat him wi' his heead in an' his legs oot, I did switch him!"

"Ah well, God rest him all road ever he offended!" We must hurry on.

The head of Great Langdale, now coming into view, provides a cosmic setting for such human antics, a tremendous amphitheatre in which the few scattered farms are lost, the mountains are at their most majestic. Like midgets we jog down the steep, winding road to the valley and the Old and New Dungeon Gill Hotels. On the way down you can see how at the head of the valley, on the left, the tongue of land called The Band projects from Bow Fell, dividing Oxendale on the left from Mickleden on the right. Up the former you climb by Hell Gill to Bow Fell, up the latter by Rossett Gill to Angle Tarn, both routes meeting on Esk Hause; thence to Scafell Pike and Scafell. Seldom has a comparatively short sentence covered such strenuous ground so blandly. There is some justification for this hey presto style. You are not likely to attempt Scafell and its Pikes (the only really tolerable nomenclature) without the aid of Messrs. Baddeley, Bartholomew and Symonds. They will leave you in no doubt as to the difficulties and rewards. The panorama also is well detailed by them. We are familiar by now with its principal features though from here it is particularly vast, and on a clear day can include Ireland across a hundred miles of sea.

Consider for a moment how that sea sweeps round the
coast giving a unity to an area which is greater than the
Lake District proper. We are on the highest point of
England, 3,210 feet high, yet the mountains go tumbling
down to the level of the sea in a dozen miles or so—an
illustration of how some of the most unforgettable and over-
whelming effects of the scenery are the result not so much of
inherent size as of the wonderful proportion that prevails
throughout a district whose greatest diameter is under thirty
miles. This is the highest but not the oldest point. There in
the north rises Skiddaw, whose name identifies the kind of
rock that rose out of a timeless sea before the eruption of
the volcanoes threw up the igneous matter that was to be
weathered into the thousand-angled and faceted mass of
these central mountains among which we stand. Down there
Black Combe thrusts out into the sea a headland made of
the older rock. The gentle, wooded countryside around
Windermere is characteristic of the Silurian rock that came
later. The surface of the earth on this mountain's top is bare
and stony. By contrast, the green vale of Esk gleams like
another Eden far below on its way to the sea. From Bow
Fell just opposite, the volcanic rock forms the far side of
the neighbouring vale of Duddon and, as we saw when we
stood on Duddon Bridge, retains its scenic characteristics
from the knobbly crest of such a mountain as Glaramara to
the last knobbly stone on which you stub your toe on the
unpredictable path. And from the last little hill of Bank
End the volcanic rock falls, and, as sand, joins all the other
sand of the Duddon Estuary, just as farther up the coast
Esk brings down its quota of pink granite to mingle with
all the rocks which the restless ocean breaks and mingles
along this coast; the endlessly variegated pebbles under the
lee of the red sandstone of St. Bees Head; the fine sands at
Seascale; or the multi-coloured shingle on which the green
and white seahorses charge and withdraw at Silecroft. Much
other matter for reflection could keep us on this mountain-
top, but once more we must seek the valley, and by Great
Langdale get ourselves to Grasmere.

When the dales were so remote that they had to be self-
sufficient, and before entertainment was mechanized and

enjoyment passive, the dalesmen devised sports which
fortunately have retained their vitality and interest both for
those out of whose daily lives and occupations they spring
and for visitors who at Whitsuntide and during August and
September can attend a variety of sports meetings and other
gatherings.

Grasmere Sports, usually on the third Thursday in August,
is the most famous of these. It is notable for a very stiff Fell
Race to the top of Butter Crags and back. To watch that is
to realize why though fell-racing retains its old popularity
this is a sport which is not for export because there are few
other places which can offer a "straight up and down" course
in full view of a sports field and few breeds of man inclined
to make sport of running up and down a mountain. Most
Lakeland sports meetings have a fell race, and whilst visitors
are holding their breath and watching the headlong descent
of grass slope, scree and crag, the dalesmen are glumly
watching the time and comparing the apparently suicidal
progress of the runners with the "fast" times of giants of
bygone days.

Grasmere is also classic ground for the Cumberland and
Westmorland style of wrestling, a sport which is increasing.
Formerly it was only a sport for the summer meetings in
the valleys, but now there are several wrestling "academies"
which wrestle indoors throughout winter. But it is in the
grass arenas at Grasmere, Ullswater, Braithwaite, Keswick,
Ennerdale, Egremont and other places that the wrestling is
at its best. In white "union" suits which cover the body
from neck to feet, and short velvet trunks, the giants wrestle
on a knock-out basis, and it is open to any man to win a
world title in the two counties, for a championship of the
Cumberland and Westmorland Wrestling Association is a
world championship. This sport is unique. Its exponents
have gone far in other fields where muscle is important.
Douglas Clark, a wrestling champion, was an English Rugby
League International for years playing for Huddersfield and
made a world-wide reputation as an all-in wrestler; George
Lowden wrestled against men from other lands and beat
most of them, and won a large collection of trophies which
now has a place of honour in the museum of his home town,

Workington. At times the world's greatest wrestlers have
been brought to Lakeland sports, to Grasmere in particular,
to try to fell the local men, but in most cases the Cumbrians
and Westmerians felled the challengers, and the fashion for
wealthy sportsmen to finance these contests has died out.
It could be that there are no more sportsmen interested or
wealthy enough to sponsor the bouts, or it could be that the
wrestlers of Cumberland are the toughest of their kind and
are recognized as that.

Another typical Lakeland sport is hound trailing. Once
upon a time this racing of hounds was carried on in a happy-
go-lucky way with a variety of hounds chasing a variety of
scents over courses which varied in length from five miles to
the gruelling 25-mile trail run many years ago near Ulverston
and won by a hound called "Ringwood", a famous name in
the sport.

The trail hounds have been developed from foxhounds of
the fell packs and bred for speed, stamina and scenting
capabilities. For up to ten miles the older hounds follow the
scent on a trail which has been laid by dragging a rag soaked
in aniseed and oil over the country, and they must cover the
distance in a time between 25 and 45 minutes. First-year
hounds, called "puppies" in hound trailing, cover a shorter
trail. There is no slap-happiness about hound trailing today.
There is a hound trailing association, and an offshoot body
called the "Border H.T.A." which govern the sport and
insist on adherence to rules. In a sport where everything,
from the slip to the end of the trail is left to the hound, there
must be safeguards against the sharp practices which could
have ruined the sport if they had gone unchecked. It is a
gambling sport, and at every trail there is a crowd of book-
makers shouting the odds and a bigger crowd of punters
laying their bets. A shilling is often the bet, but there's big
money too, and more than one hound-trailing man has
carried £1,000 away from a trail in recent years.

Bearing the gambling in mind, it is small wonder that
hound trailing was eyed by gambling "rings". They scored,
too, a few times, but the H.T.A. ordered secrecy in the laying
out of the trails, put scouts out in the country, and started
marking hounds at the start to stop any of the "wide boys"

from swopping hounds in mid-trail. Thus safeguarded and because it is inexpensive, a collier or a farm hand can own and train a champion, but it takes an experienced eye to pick a coming champion when it is still a puppy.

Grasmere and Rydal can be the quietest places on earth. They can also be the noisiest. One moment as you are walking from Loughrigg Terrace high above the lake the peace seems indestructible, the next the vale profound seems suddenly to be quite literally overflowing with the sound of a succession of motor-cycles. Or the air is filled with the more appropriate and picturesque cacophony of hunters, hounds and horns with which death comes to the fox.

But any of these are as a Quaker meeting compared to the noise-making capacity of a hound trail. The start, with fifty hounds, trained, straining to be after the trailer, is only sur-passed in noise by the finish, when an ear-splitting bedlam of shouts, whistles, screams and hunting horns is let loose as soon as the hounds come in sight for the finish. Owners and trainers are penned behind a wire, the judges, with six men to catch each of the first six hounds, concentrate. The crowd, with its money on a favourite, join in the shouting. Only the hounds are quiet; they save their wind for the finish. With the favourite in the lead—most keen hound trailers can tell the difference between hounds, but to strangers they are all alike—the noise blends into a wail of delight. And then, as likely as not, the favourite will stop, within reach of the winning tape, to take a drink at a tempting stream.

Only one sport has died, and that because the law forbids it. Cock-fighting in Cumberland was as popular as anywhere in England, and it lasted longer, "mains" being held as recently as just before the Hitler war. Like other things which are driven underground, cock-fighting flourished when its followers were dodging the law, but it was easier for a Gestapo man to join the Maquis than for the ordinary man in the street—let alone a journalist or policeman—to reach that inner circle which was allowed to know the date and place of the mains.

Although actual cock-fighting has died out the "fancy" remains, and fighting cocks are still bred—but only for

Old Dungeon Gill, Langdale ☞

shows, and every fur and feather society in the area has special classes for game birds.

The sight of Mr. Heaton Cooper's studio in Grasmere and the evocative paintings by himself and his father are a reminder of the omission of one more aspect of the many-sided subject of the Lake District. Constable and the masters of the first great period of English landscape painting did not on the whole make a success of the mountains and lakes, but there has been a distinguished succession of true observers and interpreters. We have had too many poets and not enough about the painter, such as the topographical Farington, Sunderland (who was also for a time Lord Lieutenant of Lancashire), William and Sawrey Gilpin, Amos Greene and his wife Harriet whose work can hardly be separated, William Havell, Sam Bough from Carlisle and all the others. But however huge the book on this subject it could never be said that one had "all put in that should not be left out". Here for instance is Dove Cottage, so evocative that all one can say is that no doubt you have been there and if not you are no doubt just about to go there. Most interesting and compact of recollections of Wordsworth and his family you will find it. If I let them speak for themselves it is simply to make a plea for their successor de Quincey who lived here twenty-six years after Wordsworth. Even Mr. Edward Sackville-West's first-rate biography has not wholly repaired the neglect of this interesting little genius. I will confess that had I the choice by some miraculous trick of time of a long winter evening at Dove Cottage, I would prefer the hospitality of Thomas to that of William. We would have more in common on many subjects particularly books, food, and human frailty. Wordsworth had comparatively few books; de Quincey was able to lend Coleridge five hundred at a time! And of those present on the occasion of the dinner party at Ambleside I think de Quincey would register the staggering behaviour of the hostess more profoundly than any. Let his voice be heard for once in these pages:

Our party consisted of six—our hostess, who might be about fifty years of age; a pretty, timid young woman, who was there in the character of a humble friend; some stranger or other; the

Wordsworths, and myself. The dinner was the very humblest and simplest I had ever seen—in that there was nothing to offend—I did not then know that the lady was very rich—but also it was flagrantly insufficient in quantity. Dinner, however, proceeded; when, without any removals, in came a kind of second course, in the shape of a solitary pheasant. This, in a cold manner, she asked me to try; but we, in our humility, declined for the present; and also in mere good-nature, not wishing to expose too palpably the insufficiency of her dinner. May I die the death of a traitor, if she did not proceed, without further question to any one of us (and as to the poor young companion, no form of even invitation was conceded to her) and, in the eyes of us all, eat up the whole bird, from alpha to omega. Upon my honour, I thought to myself, this is a scene I would not have missed. It is well to know the possibilities of human nature.

Dove Cottage was Wordsworth's home from 1799 to 1808. He then lived at Allan Bank for three years, at the Rectory for two, and came to Rydal Mount in 1813 to live in his fourth and last home in the district until on April 23rd, 1850, anniversary of Shakespeare's birth and death day, he died as his favourite cuckoo clock struck the hour of noon.

I have lived with him and his writings for so long, and, during the writing of this book with such renewed vividness, that I feel I almost knew him personally in life. Yet the more I know him, or imagine I do, the more incredible I find him. He was undoubtedly *the* genius loci of the Lake District. His spirit is everywhere, and it is a great enrichment of one's interest and enjoyment in the district that it should, throughout a long lifetime, have inspired a great poet, a true son and lover content to live his life out to the end in his native territory who yet achieved the status of a major poet of international fame, and a pre-eminent one in any short list of our own country. How on earth did it happen?

He never had to struggle with poverty or lack of recognition like so many poets. No tragedy of ill-health shaped or shortened his life as it did those of Keats, Lamb, Lloyd and others. No enemy within caused such internal strife as Coleridge and de Quincey endured. Both as man and poet he was truly simple. But sensuous and passionate? Sensibility, affection, emotion—yes. About what we now know of what was sensuous and passionate in his life (and there may be more still to know) he was secretive, almost furtive. Those things he kept almost as Auden said Housman kept tears, "like dirty postcards in a drawer". He was devotedly ministered to by women, who were either Martha or Mary, and, if occasion demanded, either had to be capable of being both. "William in the field all morning composing. No success. Peas for dinner," is a typical entry in Dorothy's *Journal*. In appearance, though he had something of the weather-beaten farmer about him, he was loosely-knit, stooping and awkward. He generally wore a loose brown frock-coat, trousers of a shepherd's plaid, a loose black handkerchief for a necktie, a green and black plaid shawl round the shoulders and a wide-awake straw hat, generally with a blue veil attached to it. He had a horse-like face, large nose, and, at thirty-nine looked sixty. He had weak eyes and his appearance cannot have been improved by the green goggles and broken tooth that Emerson notes. Large tracts of human knowledge and experience were closed to him. He was largely indifferent to history. He did not influence the course of events in his day, and his most enduring influence on the future lay in his abnormal capacity for remaining silent, thus foxing the critics about Annette Vallon for a hundred years and probably leaving them with still plenty to nose out about his unrecorded activities in France. Matthew Arnold's brother Thomas remembered an anti-railway meeting presided over by Prof. Wilson, at which Wordsworth, then in his late seventies, made a long, rambling, almost sentimental speech which Wilson, with unexpected business-like ability, interrupted two or three times brusquely if not rudely to make him speak to the resolution. Wordsworth wrote two passionate sonnets against the extension of the railway beginning: "Is then no nook of English ground secure from rash assault?" and ending by informing Mountains and Vales and Floods that he called on them to "share the passion of a just disdain". In a letter to Charles Lloyd he sought advice on how best to invest five hundred pounds in the new company. Would he be pleased or not, I wonder, that in the Great Hall at Euston hangs a striking picture of Dove Cottage—type of the delights the railway has to offer?

Even as a countryman, responsive to and articulate about every sight and sound of the countryside, he had no interest in agriculture, sheep-farming, hunting or any form of country sports. His rustics are projections of his own ideas, not the result of observation, affectionate or satiric. Even the pleasures of reading meant little to him. They were suitable for rainy weather (the Lake District would at least provide the opportunity). None of us who love books will ever forget that Wordsworth cut the leaves of a new volume with a buttery knife!

As a character, he must have been cold, humourless and uncongenial. There is an irresistible authenticity about de Quincey's account of Wordsworth's maddening assumption that he and his sister and one or two near to them had a corner in picturesque beauty. If anyone else even ventured an opinion about the light on the hills he would turn away or behave insultingly. He was after all exposed for a long time to the observations of gifted contemporaries and among them it was the genius of Carlyle that most illuminated his essential nature. Here is an indulgent glimpse at a dinner party at Lord Monteagle's—"large, luminous, sumptuous". (Here and in the last sentence of the next scene Carlyle wields a phrase one might have attributed to Henry James.) Wordsworth carried in his pocket a kind of a skeleton brass candlestick, in which he touched a spring, and there flirted out a small vertical green shade, which he then placed between his poor weak eyes and the neighbouring candles.

I looked upwards, [says Carlyle, the coast being luckily clear] there, far off, beautifully screened in the shadow of his vertical green circle, which was on the farther side of him, sat Wordsworth, silent, slowly but steadily gnawing some portion of what I judged to be raisins, with his eye and attention placidly fixed on these and these alone. The sight of whom, and of his rock-like indifference to the babble, quasi-scientific and other, with attention turned on the small practical alone, was comfortable and amusing to me, who felt like him but could not eat raisins.

It is a scene in which the chiaroscuro which caught the eye
of "the Rembrandt of English prose" would have delighted
Wright of Derby. In fact his last picture, a view of Ullswater,
had been painted some years previously. On another evening
he got Wordsworth on to the subject of great poets and was
surprised to find that all

> even Shakespeare himself had his blind sides, his limitations:
> gradually it became apparent to me that of transcendent and
> unlimited there was, to this Critic, probably but one specimen
> known, Wordsworth himself! The depths of his pride in him-
> self did not increase my love of him, though I did not in the
> least hate it either, so quiet was it, so fixed, *un*appealing, like
> a dim old lichened crag on the wayside, the private meaning
> of which, in contrast with any public meaning it had, you
> recognized with a kind of not wholly melancholy *grin*.

His latest critic, Mr. John Jones, distilled this by taking as
the title of his study of Wordsworth's imagination Keats's
phrase "the egotistical sublime".

If I seem to have weighted the evidence against him, it is
only to express the wonder at the solitary fact that re-
establishes his greatness, itself bumping the scale down so
decidedly as to scatter all the other considerations. It is the
fact with which, as he told Matthew Arnold, he answered
the clergyman, one of the pilgrims to Rydal Mount who
asked him if he had ever written anything besides the *Guide
to the Lakes*. Yes, he answered modestly, he had written
verse.

It is true those verses included the lines:

> Yet helped by Genius—untired Comforter,
> The presence even of a stuffed Owl for her
> Can cheat the time.

—verses which provide the very title for the classic anthology
of bad verse, and in "The Stuffed Owl" Wordsworth beats
all other competitors by several pages. The interesting thing
is that he would have done so by a much greater lead in any
anthology of good verse. It is surprising how much of it can
catch out even a well-read Wordsworthian, as I noted in the
introduction. Mr. Aldous Huxley has pointed out how, with
the disintegration of the solid orthodoxies, Wordsworth

Sty Head Tarn, looking north

became for many intelligent, liberal-minded families the
Bible of that sort of pantheism, that dim faith in the existence
of a spiritual world which filled, somewhat inadequately, the
place of the older dogmas. A Sunday walk was like church-
going; the First Lesson was to be read among the clouds, the
Second in the primroses. I think that view will prove more
transitory and superficial than Wordsworth's poetry. We
will take leave of him at his unassailable best. Nothing, he
says:

> can breed such fear and awe
> As fall upon us often when we look
> Into our Minds, into the Mind of Man—
> My haunt, and the main region of my song.
> Beauty . . . waits upon my steps;
> Pitches her tents before me as I move,
> As hourly neighbour.

INDEX

The Numerals in **heavy type** *refer to the page numbers of the illustrations.*